COLIN HAMPTON

A Cellist's Life

STRING LETTER PUBLISHING

Publisher: David A. Lusterman
Editors: Stacey Lynn and Jeffrey Pepper Rodgers
Production Director: Ellen Richman
Designer: Trpti Vanessa Todd
Production Coordinators: Judy Zimola and Chris Maas
Marketing Manager: Jennifer Fujimoto

Printed in the United States of America.
All rights reserved. This book was produced
by String Letter Publishing, Inc.
PO Box 767, San Anselmo, California 94979
(415) 485-6946; www.stringletter.com

Library of Congress Cataloging-in-Publication Data
Hampton, Colin, 1911-1996
    A Cellist's Life / Colin Hampton.
    p. cm. — (Backstage Books)
    Taped reminiscences transcribed and edited.
    Includes discography and index.
    ISBN 1-890490-35-0

    1. Hampton, Colin, 1911-1996. 2. Violoncellists — Biography. I. Title. II. Series.
ML41.H25 A3 2000
7874'092—dc21
[B]
                                        00-046314

CONTENTS

ACKNOWLEDGMENTS

It has been several years since Colin died and his ashes were interred in his beloved flaxen hills of Sonoma County, California, at the Starcross Community. This book has been a slow distillation of Colin's reminiscences, taped by him in 1986. The tapes were transcribed by Betty's Typing Service, corrected and arranged by Michelle Chattaway, and edited by Stacey Lynn. The historic photographs were enhanced by Marten Bot. The first tapes were transferred to CD by Mark Ferris and Gloria Leung.

The original intent of Colin's tapes was to provide small windows on his experiences as a musician. His commitment to music, to people, and to cultural and spiritual values was an inspiration to his students and his friends. We each hope for a person in our lives to whom we can look for guidance and direction. Colin was such a person: someone who holds the beacon of culture and sensibility so that we come to understand it and learn to hold that beacon ourselves for the generation that follows us.

I thank David Lusterman for his solid support of this project and Stacey Lynn, whose careful editing has retained the flavor of Colin's personality. I owe a debt of gratitude to those who knew that Colin was important, in particular to Dr. Anthony and Judy Lepire, Megan Dalton, Anne Crowden, Piero and Brigitte Mancini, Martina Lutz, Brother Toby McCarroll, and my family friend Bonnie Hampton.

Ian Hampton
Port Moody, British Columbia
August 2000

PREFACE

Colin Hampton, born June 6, 1911, was the younger of two children born to Jane Rolands and Frederick Hampton Smith. Frederick's father, an ostler in the Notting Hill gate district of London, died when Frederick was very young, leaving the boy, youngest of 14 children, to fend for himself. Frederick became an organist, and family legend has it that he harmonized "Keep the Home Fires Burning" for composer and actor Ivor Novello for a fee of three guineas. Jane, of Welsh farming stock, was a nurse, and her marriage to Frederick came as something of a surprise to Frederick's friends, who regarded him as a flamboyant musician and something of a wag. During the First World War, he directed *Chu Chin Chow*, the musical everybody had to see when in London. A fine amateur woodworker, Frederick directed his war efforts to making airplane propellers, which he sanded down between the shows.

The education of Colin and his sister, Isolda, was disrupted by World War I. Colin's experiences of convent boarding school and, later, Westminster Choir School were not the happiest. He took up the cello at the age of 12, and his rapid progress put thoughts of formal education aside, and in his early teens, Colin went to study with Herbert Walenn (a student of Hugo Becker), who ran the London Violoncello School, and then to the Royal Academy of Music, to which he received a scholarship from W.H. Squire.

Colin soon took over the cello position from Peter Bevan in a promising student quartet being coached by Lionel Tertis. From this point, Colin's career was set, and his life became synonymous with that of the Griller Quartet and intertwined with the lives of his colleagues Sidney Griller, Jack O'Brien, and Philip Burton.

On leaving the academy, the Grillers set up house together and worked for a year, determined to become a string quartet of exceptional quality. Their European career, off to a good, supportive start, culminated in a Carnegie Hall recital, arranged for them in 1939 by pianist Myra Hess. During World War II, the finest musical talent was called up into the Royal Air Force, where Wing Commander O'Donald found himself conducting the greatest orchestra ever assembled in England. Myra Hess established lunchtime concerts at the National Gallery, where bomb-shocked Londoners found solace in serious music within the gallery's bare walls.

The Grillers shared in this musical heroism and it doubtless contributed to their reputation as one of the finest string quartets of their day. They played with the great instrumentalists Dennis Brain, Reginald Kell, Leon Goossens (with whom they premiered Britten's Oboe Quartet at the Venice festival), and Frederick Thurston, as well as with pianists Myra Hess, Clifford Curzon, Edwin Fischer, and Hephzibah Menuhin, among others. They developed close working relationships with a number of composers, including Arnold Bax, Arthur Bliss, and Ernest Bloch.

In 1947 the Grillers were at last able to pursue their career in North America and took a position at the University of California, Berkeley. Although their duties precluded lengthy stays in England, Sidney Griller received the CBE for the quartet's work, and all four of the Royal Academy of Music alumni received a FRAM. The Grillers developed working relationships with composers Roger Sessions and Andrew Imbrie, continued to tour, and taught and coached chamber music up to the death of their violist Philip Burton in 1962.

Colin was instrumental in founding the California Cello Club, and, through the auspices of U.C. Berkeley, he invited Pablo Casals to give a series of master classes. Colin arranged dozens of pieces for cello ensembles and was a prolific writer. With the exception of an unfinished opera, his work was all chamber music and included pieces for piano, cello, and violin, and many songs. Colin, an inspiring teacher and chamber music coach, was passionate about music. His generosity was matched by his vital interest in people and concern for his students. Colin was the last surviving member of the Griller Quartet, and his death in 1996 brought to a close a tradition that focused on pure musical values and a creative devotion to chamber music.

Ian Hampton

Colin at an early age

Education of a Musician

GUV, MY FATHER, WAS ONE of the finest musicians I have known. He was self-trained and incredibly knowledgeable. As a result, I cannot remember hearing anything for the first time, which I suppose in some sense is very fortunate and in another, perhaps, has robbed me of the shock of being bowled over by a great piece. One such time, however, which I shall never forget and which laid me low for days, was hearing the great [Fyodor] Chaliapin sing *Boris Godunov*. But for all the rest, I am very glad I had the background that I did. Guv started me on the piano when I was about six. I don't remember much about the lessons—I think they just happened every week.

I was sent to boarding school at the age of five because of World War I. When the Germans began bombing London, my sister, Isolda, and I were both sent out of the city for safety's sake, and I shall never forget the appalling homesickness. Even now it makes me sweat. However, I think my parents did the right thing, as far as they could see.

I was sent to a convent school from the age of six until I was eight. I presume that piano lessons must have gone on at school; otherwise it would have been impossible for me to play by the age of eight or nine, and I certainly could play some. When I was eight, Isolde and I were sent out of London (again because of the war) to Annecy Convent, in Seaford, where we spent the next two years. And for the next two years after that, I was a choirboy at Westminster Abbey. Those were not happy years; I hated school. In fact, I hated it all the way through, though I do strongly remember the Mozart Requiem, a Palestrina work, and Bach's *St. Matthew Passion*. I loathed arithmetic. In fact, all schoolwork was a closed book to me, I think.

At the age of ten I went to the Ecole Lycée in London, where everything was taught in French. We had two classes a week in music—the ordinary sort of theory we learn and that so few children get today—and drawing. I left the Lycée when I was about 13 and spent a year studying cello privately. I was into music good and proper at that age, and we were allowed to leave school at 13. For a year I spent my time on cello and piano, and then I went to the London Cello School, which was owned and run by Herbert Walenn, who was the best teacher in London at that time. I spent a year there and then applied for a scholarship at the Royal Academy of Music. I received one when I was 15, and at 17 I joined the Griller Quartet.

Our first teacher at the academy was Lionel Tertis, a great viola player with a huge reputation in those days and possibly still to this day, though I confess I was one who could not subscribe to the fact that he was great. I found him to have questionable tastes as an artist, and this spoiled the aura for me. I remember one lesson we had on the Schubert A Minor that consisted only of the first two measures. Sidney Griller kept picking up his violin to come in, but he never had the chance. I would call that perfecting of detail perhaps a little too much.

FIRST JOBS

I was about 16 when I was offered a job at the movie house. Of course, I was still a student at the academy, and I took this job not because it was financially of any use, but for the experience. This was in the days of silent films, so there was a good deal of playing to be done, and of course a good deal of sight reading. The movie house was at Hendon, the opposite side of London from where we lived. The salary was all of two pounds a week, and it cost me one pound 18 to get there, so the profit motive was nil, but it was a valuable experience. From there I went up the scale and got a job playing entr'acte music in a horrible little theater at Kings Cross. But again, it was wonderful experience. We had a trio there, and Fred Grinke was the first violin. I got three pounds 15 a week, and I was much nearer home, so this was a big improvement.

I took every sort of work that was available and did just about everything—I made jazz records, did symphonic work, played chamber music—and I look back with gratitude for having learned how to cope with everything. I tell students who are afraid to leave school and get into the professional world that in their final year they should play everywhere they can, take whatever jobs they can to get the experience, because experience is the finest teacher of all. I think about Anne Crowden's daughter, Deirdre, whom I started on cello when she was about ten or 12. I taught her for six years, after which she went on to Bernie Greenhouse, and from there to Zara Nelsova, and from there to the St. Louis Conservatory. She played there for two years, and she came home one time and I said, "What are you going to do now?" She said, "I think I'll go back and finish." And I said, "Well, for God's sake, don't you think you should quit wasting your time?" She took my advice and did leave, and she got a job as first chair of the Scottish Ballet. The very first thing she had to play

Colin, age four, in Cornwall

was Tchaikovsky's *Rococo Variations*. What better experience could you have than that?

Our early days in the quartet were very difficult financially. We rented a house together to save money and to be able to work, and for the first few years we eked out a living. As I recall, two of us went into a promenade orchestra for a season and two of us played in a theater job, and I think two of us also made a movie. It must have been the early movie *The Co-optimists*, which did give us quite a bit of money and probably enabled us to live.

During those early years I learned the lesson of being hard to get. There was a big and influential chamber music club in London called the Chelsea Music Club, which was run by the Piggotts. They heard us play many times, but they weren't interested. They had people like [Fritz] Kreisler, [Mischa] Elman, [Pablo] Casals, and some of the big pianists, such as [Artur] Schnabel, and singer Lotte Lehmann. They had their own pet quartet, of course. One day they had a cancellation and they went to our managers, Ibbs and Tillett, and said, "We think we'll give the young English quartet a chance. Can they play for us?" Emmie Tillett looked at our calendar and said, "No, I'm terribly sorry, they can't; they're busy," and so that was that. The next year they went in again and said, "We'd like to give this young English quartet a chance. These are our dates; can they do one of them?" Again Emmie looked into our calendar and there wasn't a date that we were not playing somewhere. Then they fell over themselves to get us, and every year after that, they simply arranged their season around us. This happened right up until the beginning of the war, when it was no longer possible to get the artists they wanted for the rest of the seasons. They became personal friends, and we used to stay with them sometimes at their cottage in Buckinghamshire, which also made me realize that an artist must get away from his normal place of livelihood from time to time.

Another lesson I learned had to do with something that at first worried me greatly. There was a time that I began to feel nothing, no sense of the beauty, no sense of the emotion, even in late Beethoven and Mozart. After a while I realized that this happened when I was tired and that I shouldn't battle it. I would think, "All right, it's going to be a dull concert, and I'm not going to feel the music tonight, but just don't worry about it; that happens." Usually with a good rest I would come alive again. Similarly, I used to get tight in concerts. Especially in my youth, I would find myself getting tighter and tighter, and sometimes it was all I could do to finish a concert. I had to think, "All right, I'm not going to give a damn what happens in the first two or three minutes of the performance," and so I was able to cure this.

THE ROYAL ACADEMY

Some (perhaps most) of what I have to say about the Royal Academy of Music will be detrimental, but I feel I have to be honest and say what I think. I will say that I had a very fine education in the theoretical aspects of music—harmony, counterpoint, piano (which was compulsory, thank God, and should be in the life of every child who has anything to do with music), sight-reading, transposition (which we had to do on the piano), and so on, as well as orchestral playing and chamber music playing—for which I have been eternally grateful.

One point that was never mentioned at the academy was what music is all about, what its value is. It wasn't until we went to study a few years later with Arthur Williams that I began to get an inkling about this. Williams was a very fine cellist who had been interned in Germany through World War I. He had left England in desperate financial straits and was caught in Germany. He came back to England a rather broken man at the end of the war, and it was many years after that that we went to study with him in Wales. (I also want to mention Alex Cowan in this regard. He was the sort of man that almost nobody knew but who had a great deal of insight into music. His understanding of the whys and wherefores of music was absolutely superb.)

I went back to the academy in about 1971. I had decided I would like to go back and live in England, so I sold my house, furniture, and everything here in California and went back to teach at the academy. Unfortunately, the academy had suffered badly from always hurrying students through so that they in turn could become professors. And rather like Christ was undone by his disciples, the great are always torn down by their devoted followers.

When I went back to teach, I realized within in a month that I had made a great mistake. I remember coaching a Haydn quartet on one occasion. The first violin had a chromatic run for which she fingered open string 1, 1, 2, 2, 3, the old-fashioned chromatic scale, which sounds just like you've trodden in a pound of margarine. I said, "No, you cannot possibly do it that way." And she said, "That is the only way you can finger a chromatic scale." I responded, "Well, you better settle down and learn a new way right now." So I taught her. She came back the next week and played a perfect chromatic scale.

Then there were the cellists. When their colleagues were playing spiccato-bow eighth notes in Haydn or Mozart quartets, the cellists would

Herbert Walenn, founder of the London Cello School

be playing on the string. I'd say, "Don't they teach spiccato in this building?" And they would say, "No." They didn't know their Italian terms, which shocked me. I realized that if I were to stay there, I would make an enemy of every other teacher, and so I resigned. I called up the principal's secretary and said I wanted to make an appointment to see the principal. We made the date and then she said, "May I ask what it's about? He doesn't like to be surprised." I said, "Yes, I want to offer my resignation." And she gasped. When I met with the principal, he hemmed and hawed, but he didn't ask, "Why are you leaving?" and I didn't offer to tell him why. I would have loved to have done so, but I don't think it would have done any good; they're too entrenched in thinking they're the only people in the know. It was sad to me that going back 40 years later, I heard the Sammartini Sonata being taught in exactly the same way that I had been taught myself—all the same old fingerings, whether they went against the music or not.

When I was 17, I had found myself having to play the Brahms Clarinet Quintet with [Frederick] Thurston, who was then BBC first clarinet. There is a run by the clarinet in the first movement of this quintet (just before the recapitulation), and he was coming down so cleanly and I so messily, playing in the positions as we'd been taught—everything in positions. I hate positions. I think [Eugène] Ysaÿe was right: the *finger-board* is the position. When I went home that night, I thought, "I cannot play it this way," so I invented a system of fingering and I have never gone back to the old.

Anyway, so back I came, and I was glad to shake the dust off my feet. I'd been gone from England too long anyway. I could never have settled down there again.

MUSEUM PIECES

I had a theory that the viola should be played by cellists and not by violinists, because I could never quite understand or accept the fact that so many violas had been cut down to make it possible to play on the arm or under the chin. During the war, I read in the papers that Hills in London had given the "Messiah" Strad to the Ashmolean Museum in Oxford. I was very anxious to see it, so I wrote to the curator and we made a date, and I went out to Oxford. It was not on show, but the curator unlocked one of the galleries and said, "Come on in." I did, and he locked the gallery behind us. It was stacked up with cases of Spam and toilet paper and God knows what else. There was one chair, and he said, "Sit." So I sat, and he said, "I'll get the violin for you."

The next thing I knew, there was a dilapidated old fiddle case tearing across the polished floor, and it landed at my feet. I picked it up and took out the "Messiah" Strad. It almost looked brand new, like a modern French fiddle. The curator said, "Oh, we have some other instruments, too." And he produced three Gasparo da Salò violas, each with the original necks and fingerboards, and three Amatis, also with the original necks and finger-boards. I was intrigued to find that on the back of each one there had been a hole, which had been plugged up, so these instruments had been played hanging from the neck on chains in procession, as they used to do when they were short of voices. To my way of thinking, this is about the only way the viola should be played. However, it's not up to me, which is probably fortunate for the viola and her violists.

While I was there, the curator also showed me a set of instruments that I would have sworn were of the finest Italian make, only to find they were made locally in Oxford: a viola and two violins—unfortu-nately a gamba and not a cello—but gorgeous wood. I am always fascinated to look at instruments. They are so beautiful, and there is so much to learn.

WAR STORIES

Myra Hess once gave a concert at the National Gallery during the war in which she was playing a work by Schubert. It was the days of the buzz bombs, and one came over while she was playing. It got louder and louder and so did Myra until in the end she was not playing; she was drowning out a buzz bomb—an incredible tour de force on her part.

Myra was a wonderful figurehead during those days. She conceived the idea of having lunchtime concerts at the National Gallery early on in the war. It was interesting that during World War I people were somewhat frivolous in their choice of entertainment, whereas in World War II people were deadly serious. They wanted proper music, proper theater, Mozart operas, and so on. The gallery concerts filled this need five days a week, sometimes under great difficulties: playing without any heating in the hall, playing under the central dome, where the glass had been blown out. It wasn't very comfortable to play underneath it when it was raining.

We once gave a concert there of the First Bloch Quartet. During the first movement I kept having to screw up my bow. At the end of the movement I unscrewed it to take a look at it, and I saw that the plug had come out of it. I left the platform and went off to the artists' room to see if there was a spare bow, because I did not have one. (This was a lesson for me.) Luckily my viola player was trying out a bow, so he had a spare. I borrowed that, went back, and played the rest of the concert, and no one was any the wiser, so I didn't do too badly.

Once I was asked to man one of the entry doors at the gallery, because one of the museum people was sick. I was inside listening to the concerts when there was a commotion outside my door. I looked through the glass and there was Lady Cunard gesticulating wildly to be let in. I was very imperious, and I just turned around and took no notice. As a matter of fact, I rather enjoyed that.

We did quite a few concerts at the National Gallery during the war, and it was also about this time that we started doing some concerts with Malcolm Sargent, the conductor whose nickname was "Flash Harry," I think because he could talk off the top of his head and sound very smart, even when it was nonsense. I remember doing the César Franck Quintet with him. When he came to the silences in the first one, he said, "Let's cut these; they're so boring." We also did piano trios with him, and he would always double the bass. This went on for the first few rehearsals, and before the concert I said to him, "It's fine in rehearsal, but would you mind at the concert not doubling the bass and putting it down an octave too low?" He said, "Oh yes, yes, yes, yes, of course, you see, I'm so used to reading the score up and down." But at the concert he did just the same.

THE ROYAL AIR FORCE

If my memory serves me, the air force was run by six air chief marshals, five of whom were amateur chamber music players—a good stroke of fortune for us. Not only were we enlisted as a unit, but they created the most superb symphony orchestra, because they wanted to save all the fine young talents of the day. We were extremely grateful for this. The first year of the war when we were playing for the troops and in factories and so on, we did about 250 concerts, and we did not fall below that number for the next five and a half years while we were in the Royal Air Force. But we had very little to complain about. There were the usual troubles—lack of food, difficult transportation, no heating, and so on—but that was little enough to suffer.

RAF Band on a
bond drive in
Fort Worth, Texas

We were living on about three and six, about 50 cents a day, so those were difficult days financially. One jazz unit had 14 shillings a week taken

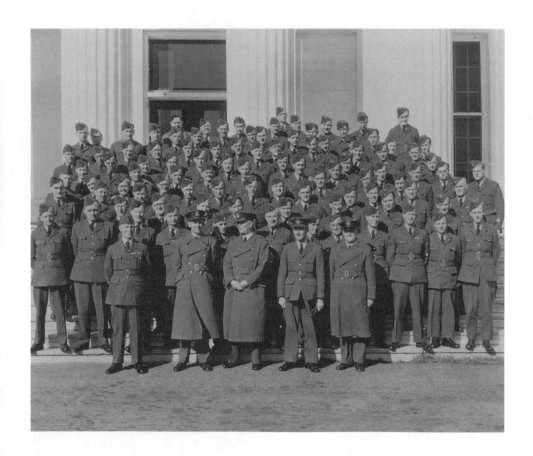

out of each airman's pay to go toward the support of his wife and family if he had one. Because of an administrative oversight, they had not taken the money out of one fellow's pay, and he was court-martialed. He was asked, "How could your wife exist without this money? Didn't she complain?" And he said, "Well, we never noticed it, sir, because I allow her 1,000 pounds a week." He used to make fabulous sums arranging jazz tunes. So nothing was done about it, and they dropped the case.

One time we played the Dvořák Piano Quintet at an officers' mess concert with Dennis Matthews, and in the middle of the first movement a wing commander came up behind me and said, "I say, old boy, would you mind keeping it down a bit? We can't hear ourselves talk." The commanding officer happened to see this, and he came up and said, "What happened?" and I said, "Well, I'd rather not say, sir." He said, "I insist." So I had to tell him. The man was made to apologize to us in front of everyone. It was very embarrassing.

The man who was in charge of the defense of London during the buzz bombs was a lovely man with a very nice family, and we were quite friendly. They asked us if we would play at the commanding base in London. It was a big concert, and Myra Hess was playing with us. Our host and hostess greeted everybody in the most affable way. They were very polite and considerate, and the evening went off beautifully. The next day we heard that their only son had been killed. It was the most incredible example of keeping a stiff upper lip I have ever seen. What it must have cost them, I have no idea, but they were extraordinary.

I recall an incident that occurred when we were to give a performance at the RAF intelligence department. Harry Blech, who was one of the better violinists in those days, was to play a Mozart Concerto. Harry had been given the nickname Waste of Space, and we always liked to tease him. So I sent a telegram in the morning to the intelligence department saying we would be late for the concert—arriving by taxi—Mozart. About a week after the concert I learned that the air force had not been able to make head nor tail of this wire and had sat decoding it for most of the day. So much for our efforts.

PLAYING AT POTSDAM

After the war, England was supposed to provide entertainment at the Potsdam Conference. About 20 of us were flown to an airfield just outside of Berlin. We were informed that it would be wise to take as much chocolate, cigarettes, and foodstuffs as we could, as this was the best currency, so we took what we could afford or what our families could spare. The first day we were there, we were taken into Berlin to see what it looked like. I didn't see one building that wasn't scarred in one way or another, and of course most of them were demolished. We wandered around a bit, and we saw where the black market was functioning. It was rather terrifying to see people clearing the rubble with their hands because they had no shovels or wheelbarrows or tools. The children looked well, but the older people looked awful. I watched for a while and saw a young pregnant woman who was holding the hand of a little girl of about five. Her old father had a face like parchment, it was so yellow, and his collar looked several sizes too large for him. I think he had been so starved that he had shrunk. As they wandered on the scene, they looked a little surprised to see the black market dealings. But then the woman took off her wedding ring and proceeded to offer it for sale. When she came over to me and offered me the ring, I just put two packets of 20 cigarettes in each hand of the little girl and refused to take the ring. It seemed to me appalling to take advantage of people in such a terrible plight, despite the fact that we had suffered so much at their hands.

Some days later we were taken by trucks out to Potsdam, which was quite an experience. For miles there were two Russians with guns about every five yards. When we arrived at what was left of Potsdam, we saw a group of kids playing on the street in front of what had been a four-story building. Just the facade was left, and suddenly there was a huge gust of wind, and we saw the whole thing topple on those kids.

We continued on up to the house where the conference was being held, and the security was incredible, including many Russian guards in boats on the river. We were stationed in an anteroom while everyone was served dinner. We saw Truman, and we saw Stalin, who spoke to us in Russian, which we couldn't understand. Stalin had the most candid eyes, and he always had a bodyguard. Churchill clearly was in a very bad mood the whole time because of the British elections going on, and he couldn't settle down. He kept sending for newspapers and listening to news over the radio and was generally a pain in the neck for everybody else. Among the many toasts at dinner was one to the meeting of the allies in Tokyo, about which we were sworn to secrecy, because this was never supposed to happen. Britain and America were determined it wouldn't happen, and of course it never did.

At one point Truman came into the anteroom, where there was a piano, and spoke with us. He was very pleasant. Then he sat down at the piano and played. I don't remember what he played, but he did it very badly, and I remarked that I hoped he would be a better president than pianist.

ON TOUR

I remember the tremendous excitement when we started to make a name for ourselves and began to travel far afield to play. That excitement lasted about ten years. Then the traveling and playing began to be a bore, and then it began to be a terrible onus, but still one did it, of course. Traveling could be dreary. Always it was the same four people together, as far as we were concerned. In Europe, especially England, people used to offer us "hospitality." There was not enough money in the clubs to put us up at a hotel, so they would cut corners by having several families each take in one member of the group. This led to some strange situations from which we were often glad to get out. I remember one hostess who talked about the "London Sympathy Orchestra" and another who wanted to clean my shoes: "You are not leaving my house with dirty shoes." She went down on her hands and knees and cleaned them, making me feel absolutely awful.

RAF Band on its wartime bond drive tour

On one occasion we were leaving Darlington for Scotland. This was our first trip up there. We knew we had to change trains at Newcastle, but we didn't realize how close to Newcastle Darlington is. We got on the train, didn't want to travel all night in our evening clothes, and wanted to change. We got out white shirts, collars, vests, and underwear when the train arrived in Newcastle, so we had to get out of the train and continue dressing on the platform. That was fun.

I once heard a good traveling story about the violinist Cyril Stapleton. He was put up in somebody's house, and he was up in the attic. There were two or three little steps outside his room to the landing, then the steep stairway to the ground floor. In the middle of the night he had a call to go to the bathroom and he thought, "I can't wander round the house." There was a chamber pot under the bed so he used that. But then he decided, "Well, I really can't sleep with the smell of this here," and forgetting the three steps outside his room, he opened the door to put the chamber pot outside, and it rolled all the way downstairs. He dressed, found his way out of the house, and left!

One of the awful things about touring was the hospitality offered in America. After a concert you are always invited somewhere and you have to go. On one occasion we were making our way from California back to New York and then back to England. Sidney's wife, Honor, had been traveling with Sidney. Instead of flying straight to England, she was persuaded by Sidney to tour with the quartet: "Come on, see how you like it." We had six weeks of touring and after two weeks, Honor said, "I'm not coming to any more of your concerts. I realize how hard you boys work. I know what the traveling is like, I know about the strain of concerts, but I had never realized how appalling the hospitality can be and what a hardship it is." We would never eat a proper dinner before a concert. We might have an egg or something at 6 P.M. and then play at 8 o'clock. By 10 or so, we would be pretty hungry and out we would have to go to somebody's house, where we might be given a piece of cake, some ice cream, and a cup of coffee. That could be miserable. Then, of course, some amateurs or young children or parents ask for advice, perhaps ask for fingerings, so we were working all the time.

This was one of the problems of summer schools. At Santa Barbara, we would breakfast at 7 A.M. with the students. The questions would begin and we would go all day long, coaching, teaching, answering questions during breakfast, lunch, and dinner and throughout the evening—unless there was a concert—then after the concert, again questions. I used to go over to my house, and kids would go with me. I would reach my bedroom door and say, "I'm getting undressed; you may stay if you like." And then they would leave. So it's not that you do two or three hours of teaching; it happens all day. This is tiring.

IN THE STUDIO

Early recording was a terrible strain. We used to do a whole day of sessions and be exhausted at the end of it. In those days we recorded on a thick piece of wax, and you couldn't play back your record. It would have to be taken off and processed, and you couldn't hear it for about three months, so you'd make four or five recordings of each side. In those days you could play for only four minutes and 20 seconds, so you would have to find a congenial stopping place, which meant that sometimes your tempos were too fast or too slow. Generally the fast ones suffered. As the day wore on, you would get tighter and tighter, and at about four minutes and ten seconds, in sheer desperation one of us would make a mistake, and we'd have to start again.

Colin at about age 16

We did quite a lot of recording during the war. Sometimes I would come across one of our recordings, such as the C-Major Mozart, which we did in a very cold spell. I don't think the pitch remains the same on any part of that record because of the overloading of electricity. We would hit a point where the electricity would drop and the sound would get sharper, and then halfway through a movement suddenly the pitch would take a dive.

When the recordings started to be done on tapes, that was a godsend. We were committed to do the Haydn Serenade, the Sibelius, the Mozart "Hunt," the third Bliss (which he wrote for us and was an extremely difficult work), and the Beethoven A Minor, Op. 132. We started with the Bliss, and to our astonishment most of the strain was gone, because they can do wonders just changing a note here and there to patch things up. We did everything in five days and then on Saturday we got together to hear what we had done that week. Bliss was there, and the studio executives had bought bottles of gin, vodka, scotch, sherry, and so on, because we had worked so fast. After the first half of Bliss, we all had to have a drink, and so it went. We listened to the Beethoven last, and I noticed that in the slow movement, in the first two sections, they had left out three chords, and they asked us, "Can we record it now?" We had no music with us, but we did have our instruments, and we were leaving for New York on Monday, so it was our only chance. So we went down to the studio, and it took us about an hour to get those three chords together. I think that is very good proof that drinks and fingers do not mix. That became a rule of mine during my professional life—I never had a drink until my work was finished.

We recorded with London FFRR, but as we spent more and more time in America, we spent less in England, and in the last two or three years the only time we could get there was in the winter. They closed their studios, so we had to break our contract with them, and they took every record we had made off the market.

Recording is so much easier these days than it used to be. When we did the "Hunt" quartet of Mozart, we played it through straight, and it was fine except the two violins were not quite together on their pickup. We went to the listening box to hear it and we said, "Oh, we'll have to do it again," and the engineer perked up his ears and said, "What is wrong?" We told him the two violins were not quite together, and he said, "Oh, is that all?" He proceeded to find the spot and take off a tiny slice of tape; the violins were then perfectly together.

When I was in Vancouver, [my son] Ian went to do a recording. It was just Ian himself, just one part, I suppose to be fitted into a lot of other parts. This was the first time I'd been in a recording studio for about 25 years and I was absolutely shocked. First and foremost whenever he played, he played his single line and the engineers did something with the enormous amount of equipment they had, making it sound like a cello section. Then they asked him to do the same thing an octave higher, which he did, and again it came out like a section. It began to sound like an orchestra, and if you follow the thinking through, a handful of players could play a symphony. This is probably what is going to happen, because orchestral music is getting too expensive, and orchestras are failing left, right, and center. I have visions of going to Carnegie Hall to a symphony concert. There will be a whole mass of machinery on stage and one engineer, and we shall hear a symphony done by one man this way, and when it is over we will rise and give that engineer a standing ovation, as is usual over here, and go home. Certainly it seems to be heading this way because the big corporations don't seem to be coughing up the money, and so what are we going to do? I don't know.

IN REHEARSAL

We used to hold public rehearsals, although I never really had any patience with them—one can't behave naturally, and you accept that and hope no one notices. One year when we were at the Music Academy of the West, my billet was the hospital. I had the kitchen and the icebox, and if people wanted to come in for food afterward, they just came in and helped themselves. We had some cheese in the icebox that was a wonderfully smooth and soft cheese to eat, but God help you if you got anything on your fingers, because it would take about four days of washings to get it off. We had been rehearsing in the school hospital, and Philip had left his viola there overnight. Out of devilment I took a little bit of the cheese and put it under his tailpiece and put the viola back in the case. I told Sidney the next morning, and here we were sitting with all these students around us, having a public rehearsal. Philip didn't say anything, and Sidney was beside himself. After nearly two hours of rehearsing, he couldn't stand it any longer, and he asked, "Philip, don't you notice anything?" Philip responded, "What do you mean, notice anything?" And Sidney said, "Colin put some cheese on the tailpiece last night! Haven't you noticed it, that horrible smell?" Philip said, yes, he had, "and here I'd been thinking all morning that this is the last time I can wear sandals."

One time we did a public rehearsal here on the Berkeley campus because we were going to rehearse Roger Sessions' last quartet. It's an extremely difficult, discordant piece. We thought if we announced we were rehearsing Sessions that nobody would come to rehearsal, so we put down Haydn and Sessions. We started with Haydn, which we rehearsed for about 20 minutes, and then we started on the Sessions. Within ten minutes there wasn't a soul in the hall. I suppose it is nothing new for people to show their feelings. I have heard that the very first performance of the Debussy quartet in England had the audience in stitches, and I can remember Bartók playing his piano and percussion piece in Queen's Hall, and people were openly rocking with laughter. I think their manners are rather atrocious. Audiences certainly can be strange.

It's important for an artist, or anyone really, to leave troubles in the work room. I speak from firsthand experience of the trials and tribulations of quartets, whose life is not an easy one. Disagreements arise. Our first violin, Sidney, was not the easiest of people, and I learned early on that it was going to spoil my life unless I could forget it as soon as I left the room, and I schooled myself in this. Our viola player, Philip, could not do it, try as he would, and he used to take it home. It would wreck his pre-dinner drink, it would wreck his dinner, and it would wreck the evening for him. He would talk and talk and talk about it. I think that one of the reasons he committed suicide was that it became such a terrible problem for him. That's an oversimplification, of course, but he did attempt it three times.

The first time was so awful. It happened during the second Music Academy of the West in 1948. I had gone to bed, and suddenly I was aware of Sidney kicking my door and yelling, "For God's sake, get up!" I did, of course, and found that Philip had taken handfuls of sleeping pills. He'd thrown them all over the floor, and it was a terrible mess. We were miles from a doctor, so one of us had to rush over and wake the house mother and get her to drive us down to the local doctor in Carpenteria. We'd called him and alerted him, got Philip in a blanket, and wrapped blankets around ourselves over our pajamas. The doctor gave him a shot of something, and in the meantime he'd alerted the hospital in Santa Barbara, which was about 15 or 20 miles away. He told us, "Keep him awake, whatever you do. Burn him with cigarettes, hit him and pinch him, but keep him awake." So we did, and we got him to Santa Barbara.

We didn't know the outcome for many hours, but it was beginning to get light, and we thought one of us had better get back to school. I was chosen to go back and act as though nothing had happened—"Somebody was sick and they went to the hospital." I shaved, got dressed, had breakfast, and started the classes. We had agreed that they wouldn't call me unless the suicide attempt was successful and Philip died, so when I was suddenly called to the telephone, you can imagine my feelings. But they had called to say that he'd pulled through and was going to be all right. I wouldn't want to live through that sort of experience again. When I was called to the telephone I was coaching the Debussy quartet, and I can never hear that piece without reliving that experience.

You can be in the middle of a terrible row and have a concert coming up, and you'll have to play, but you really can't play great music with hatred in your heart. It's not possible. Many times the cause of a quarrel was forgotten in a concert, which was just as well. Nevertheless, as one gets older, quarreling can take its toll. It becomes harder to drop back to where you were. One is slower, and the hurts go deeper. Altogether, a quartet has a difficult life—not one I would wish on others. Many students say they want to become chamber music players, and frankly I don't know if I want to say, "Do it" or "Don't do it." It would be terrible to have to miss the pleasures and the incredible insights one gets into the composers' emotions and the beauty they pass down to us because one is afraid of the trials and tribulations. If I had my life to do over again, I would do the same thing.

The Grillers (Philip
Burton, Colin Hampton,
Jack O'Brien, Sidney Griller)
with Hephzibah Menuhin,
Wellington, New Zealand

Great Players

2

HAROLD BAUER WAS A GREAT PIANIST. He came from a family of four children—three sisters and one brother—each of whom played both piano and violin. Our first contact with them was after we played Op. 95 (Beethoven) at Wigmore Hall. A woman came around to me and planted herself in front of me like a tiny little dot and said, "Why do you make so many accents?"

I replied, "Because the music is strong, and the accents help make it strong."

And she said, "Only if you keep the sound up after you have made the accent." Of course, she was absolutely right. This was Harold Bauer's sister, Gertrude Hopkins, whom everyone called by her nickname, Hoppy. We became firm friends.

Hoppy ran a music club in London, which met every Sunday night at 9 o'clock in a huge room with space for about a 100 members and four Steinway grands. Sometimes we played with Hoppy during the week, but as we attended more of the concerts, we began playing there at the club.

After a few months, Hoppy began to be very rude to me. One night she stung me so badly that I said, "God, you're a bad-tempered, bloody old bitch, aren't you, Hoppy?!" A great smile spread across her face and she replied, "I've been trying to make you say that for weeks." Apparently she thought I was altogether too polite and acting too much the perfect gentleman and that this sort of behavior does not suit a performer. We remained perfectly wonderful friends, in fact, until the day she died.

Harold used to come over from the States, where he lived, and we would play with him every year. It was always a great experience. I remember playing the Schumann Quintet (naturally, of course, it would be the Schumann, though we did play other things, such as César Franck), and Harold would play the Scherzo so fast that we'd miss our entry, which was a delightful experience, as playing with him always was. He had a terrific sense of power and freedom in music.

Bauer had a great sense of humor. He once said to us after a concert, "Boys, the playing is wonderful. I really have to hand it to you. But there is only one criticism I would have to make." We said, "What's that, Harold?" because we would certainly pay attention to what he had to say. He replied, "The tenor and bottom are too heavy for the upper registers, the two violins." We said we would certainly give that due consideration. And he said, "I wouldn't if I were you because my hearing is going at the top."

One night after the coffee-and-cheese intermission at the club, Bauer went to one of the pianos and started playing Beethoven's Op. 59, No. 1. Immediately the sisters hurried to the other three pianos and joined him, and they played the whole quartet from memory without a note of music. That is what I call being a first-class musician. I wonder how many people could do that today; I don't think we have this sort of training anymore.

We called the club the Music Circle, and that is where I played with Mischa Elman when I was 17. Very few programs at Hoppy's were ever settled in advance. We would wait until 9 o'clock and see who came into the room. Elman came a few times, Kreisler came, Casals came—all the greats. One of the members of the circle was Montague Chester, who loomed quite large in our and other musicians' lives. The reason Bauer had become a pianist was that he had asked Chester whether he should be a violinist or a pianist, and Chester had said, "A pianist of course." So Bauer became a pianist. Chester couldn't play himself—couldn't read music at all—but he did have insight into good music making and knew instinctively what was right. [Alfred] Cortot, [Jacques] Thibaud, and Casals became a trio because Chester got them together. He was friends with all the greats. Chester lived in Paris and was the *Daily Mail* advertising manager for the Paris edition of that paper. Verts Agency, which was big in Paris at that time, said to him, "Chester, you run our concerts for us. You know more about music than we do."

Later when Casals and I got together to talk about old times, we always spoke warmly about Montague Chester, who by the way was the rudest man I ever met. I remember one night at Hoppy's studio, a quartet had given a performance of two of the last Beethoven quartets, and a fussy little lady went up to Chester, who was sitting in an easy chair, and said to him, "I don't know what it is, Mr. Chester, but I don't seem to get on very well with these late Beethoven quartets." Chester got himself out of his chair (which wasn't easy, because he was a very heavy man), put his hand on her shoulder, and said, "Madam, it doesn't matter."

We saw Hoppy whenever we could—always on trips back to England from the States, which began to be further and further apart. One time after we had been away a whole year, our second violinist, Jack O'Brien, thought it would be nice to see Hoppy, who then lived in Welwyn Garden City, having given up her studio and club because of the war. He didn't write or phone; he just went to her house and knocked on the door. She opened the door and said, "Who's the greatest composer in the world?"

Jack replied, "Mozart."

And Hoppy said, "All right, you can come in."

She was breathtakingly refreshing, and to me this is the hallmark of a real musician.

PABLO CASALS

It was a great privilege for me to be friends with Pablo Casals for about 25 years. Over the years, we discussed many things, and he had a wonderful way of working. When Casals had a new work to learn, he would spend a month with the score, and only then would he take the score to the piano, where he would spend another month, and when he had decided what he wanted to do with the music, what he felt it was about, only then would he take up his cello.

Many times I have thought about this and how little attention we typically pay to what the composer really wants. I used to play a little trick when I was teaching at Berkeley. Sometimes I would have a piece for the students to read, and when they were about ten measures from the end of the first movement, I would make my way to the window. The moment they finished playing I would say, "Hey, come and look at this." They would rush over to the window and then I would ask them what were the key and time signature of the piece, and they never knew.

In the Beethoven cello sonatas there are places where people play exactly against Beethoven's wishes because they do not look into the music closely enough. It's very easy to think you have it, and then when you look again you find so many things you've missed, which is a danger of always practicing from memory. Once or twice a week, one should take a look at the music. In the Beethoven piano sonatas, for example, you can see the indications that Beethoven has given to nearly all the movements. He's right every single time. And yet, we see *allegro* and *andante*, and we do only that and we don't read further, which is a great shame.

When I was a student, I was taught that when you practice trills, you should practice with a very hard, smashing down finger, and I never could trill at all. One day I asked Casals, "How do you trill?" And he said, "Well, the finger that is on the fingerboard—keep it down firmly and just flutter with the other finger. Don't bother to press the string all the way to the fingerboard, but play your note a little bit sharp so that it sounds right." After about ten minutes of trying this I had the trill for the rest of my life, and I never got tired doing it that way.

One summer Bonnie [Hampton] was working in Vermont at [pianist] Rulolf Serkin's school, and I went along on vacation. I dropped in to see Casals one night, and he said, "Oh, I'm so glad you've come." It seems that Serkin had given him a reprint of the *Geselleschaft,* and one of the books contained a letter written by one of Bach's students to one of Bach's sons. The student was describing a lesson he'd had with the great Bach that day and the enormous lengths that Bach had gone to to try to get him to play rubato—which of course is the exact opposite of what the schools (in this country, anyway) teach us. And Casals said, "I feel vindicated, because all my life I have been accused of being much too romantic in my playing of Bach." Of course when you think about Bach, of all things he was human; he must have been quite a romantic, a very emotional man. Think of the vast power at the beginning of the *St. Matthew Passion.* I got Casals to come to the University of California to teach for a month once, during which time he very much wanted to go to the top of Mount Tamalpais.

It seems that many years earlier, Lillian Hodghead and Ada Clement, who ran the conservatory of music in San Francisco, were approached by a friend who told them about a cellist making his way up from South America who was trying to raise money to get himself back to Europe. They put on a concert for him, and after they had been playing for a while, they turned to each other and said, "What has God sent us?" It was Casals. He stayed in Berkeley for about six months. The professor of Spanish, who lived on Tamalpais Road, had a huge studio in which Casals lived until he got enough money to move on. Curiously, this was the studio I also rented my first five months of living in the Bay Area, and I felt privileged to have it.

Many wonderful events occurred during our years of friendship. Only once did I hear him say something even slightly derogatory about a person—although he was strict, he was always kind. On that occasion, we were driving to San Francisco for the evening, and he was in a rather jovial mood, talking about various friends. One name that came up was Nellie Melba, the great Australian singer, and he said, "Oh, what a wonderful voice she had. It was absolute perfection." Then he started to laugh and said, "But she was such a fool."

Casals was strict, and this showed sometimes in his teaching—though he always had right on his side. Once a woman came up in a class to play the slow movement of a piece, and he let her play through it to the first

section, then he stopped her and gave her a little lecture with great seriousness about her intonation, saying what a crime it is to go on perpetrating a sin—which playing out of tune was. I think he felt strongly because it was the C-Minor Sarabande, a piece he felt extremely deeply about. I've heard him play it several times, always with great seriousness and uncellistic playing (I must admit I hate cellistic playing).

Casals during class at Hertz Hall, Berkeley

The month Casals was here at the University of California in 1960, he taught three classes, for three hours each, every week. He was superlative. One of the things I remember was that nobody played an F that he liked. Always the F's were too high for him. I think I was guilty of the same thing, because I took everything he said seriously, and so I came to the conclusion that he was right—nearly everybody's F's were too high. The trouble is, if you play an F with an open A string above it, you have to change it.

He was strict but always kind, a very wonderful mixture of both. Once Bonnie and Janet Guggenheim were playing the F-Major Brahms Sonata, which he liked very much until they came to the Scherzo. They played as is the way in America, and possibly Europe, where in general the speed of life has become faster and faster. The tempo for him was much too fast, and of course it does make more sense if it's slow. And Casals commented that when Brahms writes *allegro*, he means it by the eighth note and not the quarter.

One morning the Lalo Concerto was on the agenda. We had been to get him, as was the usual way, and he was warming up behind the scenes.

Casals festival at
Perpignan, France

We got his cello out and tuned it up, rosined his bow, which he wanted done in the most curious way (four downward strokes and that was all), and I gave him his cello. He began playing away, using the most phenomenal techniques, which one was never conscious of when he was on the concert platform. He said, "What is on the agenda this morning?" And I replied, "Among other things, the Lalo Concerto." A big smile came over his face and he said, "I haven't played that for 35 years," and yet there wasn't one moment when he could not pick it up the way he wanted, exactly where he wanted. What a wonderful example of really knowing a piece of music. (Incidentally, I found that the best way to help people learn something from memory is to have them write it out from memory first. If they can write it out, they'll know it.)

In one of Casals' classes, there was a girl from Utah who had sent a tape of Bloch's *Schelomo*, very excellently played, with piano, of course. I was one of the three judges on who should be admitted to the class, and on the grounds of the tape, we took her in, only to find once she got here that she could scarcely play at all, which put us in a terribly embarrassing position—but one that Casals understood. It must have been somebody else's tape, because she couldn't even play a movement of a Bach Suite, but Casals handled the situation with great compassion. He took one look and knew that there was something wrong with the girl. He said afterward, "I only had to look at her face once and I knew that she was a very sick girl." She played a few measures, and he said, "Ah, well, let me play it for you." He proceeded to play—this was the C-Major Suite "Courante"—and he showed her exactly what he did. He played it for her up to time, and he played it for her slowly, showing exactly how he coped with the different lengths of notes, and in the end he didn't let her play at all. He said, "Well, you see, there it is." And he called the next student. He handled this girl the same way every time she came up to play. He was a man of great understanding.

During this month, one of his sayings, which became almost a password, was "freedom with order." He found the students here played much too metronomically for his liking, and he wanted both a certain amount of rubato and the freedom of feeling. In all, this was a wonderful month, and Casals came back again two years later.

Once, after Casals had been in Japan and was coming through San Francisco, an old friend of his, Mrs. Jelenko, called me up and asked if we would like to go meet him and stay at her club with him for a couple of nights. Of course we jumped at the opportunity and went to meet him at the airport. He was arriving at about nine at night, and I suppose because I was excited to see him, I never checked to see if the plane was on time. We got to the airport only to find that the plane would be six hours late. Mrs. Jelenko went to the airport hotel, and I said, "Well, I'll wait, and when he comes in, I'll call you." When she came back at 3 A.M., his plane came in and he was the last one off. He and his wife, Martita, were walking very slowly. The concourse was crowded, and he and Martita had their heads down, not looking up at all. They must have been very tired; he was in his 80s then. Suddenly he saw our feet and looked up and said, "You poor darlings, you must be so tired."

Strangely enough, about a month later I was at the airport again, this time to meet a friend who was flying in from the Pacific Northwest. His plane had been delayed an hour, and he came off and saw me and put his cello down, and he held out his hands and said, "How can I play, I'm so tired!" and I thought of the difference between these two.

When Bonnie went to study with him in Prades, I said, "May I come for the lessons?" and he said, "Not to the first one. You can come afterward." So I went afterward. He taught in his bedroom, where he had a bed, a grand piano, and just enough room for two cellists to sit, and that was about all. I had to sit on his bed, and so for the first time I was able to see his bow hold from behind. I had always had a suspicion that he played with more or less a straight thumb on the bow, and I was right. There was nothing he couldn't do with it, though; that's why his nickname was King of the Bow.

One time I was watching David Soyer [of the Guarneri String Quartet] have a lesson with Casals on one of the Bach Suites at Marlboro. David was a grunter, and he grunted all the way through the prelude. Casals also was a grunter; it was one of the things he had never been able to cure himself of. I thought, "Is he going to tell David he mustn't make noises like that, or is he not?" Then I thought, "Of course he's not, because he can't," and he didn't. And David is still a grunter to this day.

After Bonnie had played Brahms during one of his lessons, Casals ended the class early. He was obviously very uncomfortable. He left the platform, left his cello there, and Martita went after him. I followed, picked up his cello, walked off stage, and found he was having a small heart attack. I packed up his cello and we took him back to his hotel. Martita and Bonnie went out, and I babysat with him until he had a nap and got up feeling fine again.

After his big heart attack, he was not allowed to perform Brahms for some time. He was advised by Dr. White, a heart specialist, not to do so. He didn't, but he felt this music so deeply. After his last illness he was in the hospital in San Juan, Puerto Rico, and he was in a coma for a long time, perhaps two weeks. Martita, smart and lovely girl that she is, had a tape machine there with a tape of Brahms' Fourth Symphony ready to play should he come round. Eventually he did, and she popped on the earphones and started the tape. He started to conduct, and he died like that,

which was of course the most wonderful way for him to go, because his whole life had been music.

I look back upon my days and my hours with Casals with great joy and happiness, a feeling of good fortune. Early on when we started the Cello Club here in Berkeley, I wrote to Casals and asked if he would be our patron. He wrote back and said he would be very pleased to accept, and he remembered exactly the program we had played when he last heard us some years before, which was quite an occasion for us, especially because Casals had not been in England for about 20 years, since before the war. When he was finally able to come, he played at the Albert Hall, a concert I shall never forget, starting with the Schumann, then an intermission, and then the Elgar. There must have been 10,000 people in the hall, and in one second there wasn't a dry eye in the place. He came out after the Elgar and played an encore, the slow movement of the Fifth Bach Suite.

Colin (carrying Casals' cello) arrives with Pablo and Martita Casals for master classes, Berkeley, California

MYRA HESS

Myra Hess was a wonderful musician and a good friend. On one occasion we were rehearsing the Dvořák Quintet, which we had to play in New York. In the last movement there's a silent beat that always feels like a kick in the pants. In the rehearsal, for the hell of it I pulled my C string over the bridge and played hard with the bow, setting off an appalling buzz. Myra didn't know what it was and she cracked up.

Myra once somehow got in touch with Sir Stafford Cripps, Chancellor of the Exchequer, and invited him to her home for dinner. The very first thing she did was put a whoopie cushion under him, and she sat him on it straight off. A very warm friendship developed from there. Myra was like that. We used to play the Elgar Piano Quintet with her quite often, and she swore that one time she went to sleep in the slow movement. Once she gave a recital at Queen's Hall, early in the war, and during the concert she had a severe attack of appendicitis. She stuck it out and finished the concert. An ambulance was brought to the stage door, and she was taken off

Myra Hess playing at a lunchtime concert at the National Gallery in London during World War II

and operated upon. When her secretary went to see her, Myra had just been given an enema. Her secretary said to her, "Well, Myra, I suppose you feel as if the bottom has dropped out of your world," and Myra replied, "No, I feel the world has dropped out of my bottom."

REGINALD KELL

We played a lot of concerts with the clarinetist Reginald Kell, who was a wonderful player. He was quite different from the tradition of English clarinetists, the Drapers, with whom we played many times. We were students with Kell at the Academy and when we all went our ways, he ended up in an orchestra as first clarinet, and he became a big name. Kell was a typical Yorkshireman, very down to earth and honest. He was outspoken but always a nice man underneath. He came over here and made a huge reputation for himself, and rightly so, I believe. We went with him from here to the Edinburgh Festival, and Reggie came into our room the morning after the concert with a newspaper in his hand and said, "I feel as if somebody has hit me over the head with a baseball bat." The review had been somewhat critical of his playing, and he was completely taken aback; he had not had this happen before. Of course there was a time in England when, if you made a success in America, you were blackballed in your own country, and he realized there was something of this in it. I don't think this would happen today.

Reg lived on the East Coast, and he was hounded by Benny Goodman. Benny was taking lessons from him, and if Benny had a concert to play, he would insist on seeing Kell in the morning and having Kell choose his reeds and hear his pieces. He latched on to Kell in such a way that he began to make Reg's life a misery. Reg even moved to Aspen to get away from Benny, but Benny would fly out to see him.

On one occasion, Kell came out here to do the Mozart Concerto with the San Francisco Symphony and was going to play a chamber music concert with us here on the university campus. He brought his wife out, a very nice person indeed. It turned out that he had left his music back in Aspen, so he borrowed a score from me. He said, "Please don't tell my wife I've left my music. She'd be so upset!" He would not let her know; he would rather suffer alone than put her through the torture. Another time, we hadn't played with Reggie for three or four years, and we had a concert in Ann Arbor. We flew out the day before and met about lunchtime for a run-through of the Brahms and Mozart quintets. He said, "Well, Colin, I've played this before. It shouldn't take us long." It wasn't true, of course. But he was a very nice man, and we liked him very much.

THE DRAPERS AND LEON GOOSSENS

The Drapers were wonderful clarinet players and also very nice people. We did a concert with Mr. Draper once at South Place. We were playing Brahms' Clarinet Quintet, and it was late on Sunday night. After the slow movement, he got up out of his chair, walked around the quartet, took out his watch, looked with horror at the time and said, "Come on, boys, let's hurry up before they close."

We did a tour with them in Scotland and, again in the Brahms slow movement, we were taking the lead-in quietly, and more quietly, and Mr. Draper was going to make an absolutely superb entry. He looked up as far as he could and gave us a wink, and blew, and nothing came. He was very funny about this. We went back to the hotel and had some food and some beer, and after awhile he was sitting around in his long johns, and the party was getting fairly wild. We went around to the various rooms where the shoes had been left outside the doors to be shined, and we mixed up all the shoes. For weeks after that, we got telegrams asking about the shoes.

A gathering of cellists: André Navarra, Zara Nelsova, Milos Sadlo, Adolfo Odnoposoff, (unknown), Maurice Eisenberg, Mstislav Rostropovich

During the war we produced a clarinet quintet of Gordon Jacob in Wigmore Hall that had a lot of variations. Draper felt there was one

variation too many, so at rehearsal that morning he said, "I think I'm going to go to the pub and see if I can't get rid of that variation." Sure enough, by the time we went to the hall that evening, that variation had been lifted out.

I must mention [Leon] Goossens, who was a wonderful artist. He was a very nice man as well as a very vain man. He was vain about his figure, and quite by accident I discovered that he wore a corset. I think he loved getting into his military uniform. One day a year he would dress up in it and sally forth. I suppose he had been petted and made a fuss of all his life, so he had his share of conceit. We did many, many concerts during a tour of Scotland with him once. The first concert was in Aberdeen, and he played extremely well. We started with the oboe quartet of Mozart, then played 132, and after the intermission we played the Arnold Bax quintet. It was a prime evening, and the concert was very good. We went off stage and just as we were going back to take a bow, he said, "Oh, boys, I'll take this one alone." So out he went and afterward we went out with him. The next night it was the same program, but he didn't play quite so well. At the end he said, "Come on, boys," but we held back and let him go on. He turned around to acknowledge us, but we weren't there, and he never did that to us again.

MSTISLAV ROSTROPOVICH

When the great cellist [Mstislav] Rostropovich came to Berkeley in the 1950s, he gave his first concert in the gym. He spoke no English at that time, but we invited him and his accompanist, Dediukhin, to dinner after the concert. They were wonderful people. They started to wrestle, and Slava had Dediukhin on the floor, and we had great fun.

The next time he came, he played with the San Francisco Symphony, and we arranged to have a reception for him at the Conservatory of Music. We picked him up after the concert and took him to his hotel on the way to change. We had a girl with us who had been a student at Mills College. Slava was always a bit susceptible to nice females, and Sally was a beautiful girl, vivacious and bright. Slava had an interpreter because he still spoke no English, and he asked Sally about herself. She told him she was a student at Mills, and he wanted to know what Mills was. She said, "Well, it's a small college of about 700 students, all girls." He looked very pleased and he said, "How on earth can you choose?"

That night he didn't play cello, but he did play the piano. He was a wonderful pianist, and he played a couple of his own compositions. This was the start of a very lovely friendship that has continued all these years. Once he did a master class at Berkeley three mornings in a row for which we ferried

Jack O'Brien, Philip
Burton, a student,
Sidney Griller, and
Colin Hampton in
California, 1948

him back and forth from San Francisco, where he always stayed. On the way back one morning he was very quiet. Nancy Adler, a very warm and friendly person, was with us, and she asked, "Why do you do so many concerts, Slava?" He said, "Because it stops me from thinking about Russia."

I discovered that he knew his itinerary for at least the next four years. He could tell you where he was going to be, the dates he would be there, his flight times—nearly everything. I have never seen such a memory.

One time I asked him to come for dinner, and Megan [Colin's third wife] and Ian went to pick him up. Sometimes he was very talkative on these drives, and sometimes he was very silent—either lost in thought or just dozing—and we didn't disturb him. This night he was lost in thought and didn't say a word on the drive over. He brought his little dog, Pooks, with him, and as I had not locked our dog out, there was very nearly a dogfight as he came in. We got the dogs separated, and the first thing he said was, "Paper. I want paper." I asked, "Writing or manuscript?" He wanted music paper. On the way over he had written the cadenza to the Haydn D-Major Concerto and he wanted to put it onto paper as soon as possible.

Bonnie was there that night, and she asked him, "Why do you take such fast tempos?" He said, "Well, it's the fashion of today, and I think one should go with it." I disagree with this. I think it is up to the giants to show us the way, and not to concede to public opinion. For example, Heifetz' recital programs could be devastatingly awful. He would usually start off with a good classical work, and the rest would be dross. Yet he was the only person who could have given first-class recitals of the sort that [Joseph] Szigeti used to do. Once when Slava played a recital, he finished with a piece of his own as an encore, and when I went in to talk to him afterward he said, "Oh, that's such a difficult piece." I replied, "Slava, you've only got yourself to blame for it," which he thought was funny.

The cellists' club on campus put on a big potluck supper reception for him once, and we picked him up as usual. Several people came up to me and said, "Wasn't it wonderful talking to him? What did you talk about coming in from the city?" I replied, "Water beds," which was exactly what we had talked about. I think we shocked some older members of the Cello Club. However, I am sorry to say that Slava has not been here for quite a few years now and apparently will not come while our critic Robert Commanday is here. They seem to have had some sort of falling out. Commanday does say rather bad things about Slava's conducting, but I think it would be wise of Slava to ignore it. In any case, one should listen to criticism, because sometimes a person with no knowledge or training can put his finger on something, so it is worth considering. In the meantime, Slava's absence has deprived us of some great cello playing.

WILLIAM PRIMROSE

I knew Bill Primrose on and off for about 30 years. The first time I met him was down at Dartington [southeast England], and he was with Dorothy, his first wife, who later died of cancer. It was an extremely happy marriage. Bill was something of an enigma. I think he had no sense of humor, and he didn't altogether seem the stuff that most musicians are made of. He seemed to be terribly talented and a "good boy." He was always very nice. Bill was a rather unimportant violin soloist, a Glasgow boy who would come to London perhaps once a year and perform a Mendelssohn or something and do very well, but it was nothing that would shake the world. He would get a good review and then he would return to Glasgow. But then he took up the viola, and I have never seen such a change in anybody. It was a wonderful example of someone who had taken up the wrong instrument, an instrument that did not reflect his personality. This could be an enormous subject for someone to write a book about. From the moment Bill gave his first viola recital, he was top of his field. If you've ever heard the *Eyeglass Duet,* the recording he did with Piatigorsky, you'll see that it almost makes Piatigorsky sound like a baby. Somehow the violin never quite suited Bill.

Bill Primrose is not the only person who initially took up the wrong instrument, by the way. Years ago, the second year we were in Santa Barbara, we met a violinist from Salt Lake City. This girl had no character in her violin playing; it was blah in every way. We said, "Sally, you are on the wrong instrument. You should be on the viola." We found a viola for her, and about a week after that we had to drive up from Santa Barbara to Berkeley, where she was. We did two viola quintets with her, and she was very good. Shortly after that she became first viola of the Salt Lake City Symphony.

I have seen this happen several times. Anne Crowden has a student, a little girl who is 11 years old and very bright. When she plays the violin, she sounds exactly like a viola. I've said to Anne, "You really have to change that child eventually." Anne doesn't want to yet, because she says the girl will learn more technique on the violin, which is true, I think.

In any case, we did several concerts with Bill Primrose, viola quintets and sextets, usually with Nicolai Graudan, who was a good cellist and a very nice man. If there was a big game on, Bill would rehearse with a radio underneath his stand, turned down. Every time we paused, he would bend down to hear what the score was and then continue on. It was very curious. I remember meeting Bill on one occasion in London that stuck in my mind. It was a gray, cold summer morning, and I was walking through Swiss Cottage quite early on a Sunday when I bumped into him. We started chatting and I asked, "What on earth are you doing over here, Bill?" And he said, "I'm here for the good of my soul!" in a very sepulchral voice.

Bill made some interesting observations. Once we were rehearsing Mozart's C-Major Quintet, and Bill turned to my colleagues and said, "I like the way your cellist plays these runs best—better than the rest of you." That riled Sidney in particular, and he asked, "Well, what does he do differently?" Bill answered, "Well, he uses his left hand like Heifetz does. He throws his fingers with his hand. And when he comes down, he does left-hand pizzicati." I was completely unaware that I did this, so this was news to me, but my colleagues were not very happy with that.

This rehearsal was during the time that we were going to record the Mozart viola quintets. It was two weeks before Christmas, and Bill had driven out in their Cadillac with his family. They had a little boy and a little girl, and Bill ensconced his family in the Claremont Hotel. We proceeded to rehearse for a week and then we began the recording in a high school in Redwood City, about 30 miles south of San Francisco. We were having a particularly bad winter, one rainstorm after another. Bill wouldn't drive down with us every day; he liked to drive himself, so we drove down in two or three cars. It continued to pour, not letting up. Every day the floods got worse, and we were driving through higher and higher water. Bill's temper was getting worse daily, and his wife and kids were stuck in the hotel all day without transportation. Things became strained because he was rather strained.

Christmas fell on a Sunday that year, and we finished our recording at lunchtime on Saturday. We came home, and I said to Bill just before we left, "By the way, Bill, what are you doing for Christmas?" He replied, "Oh, I don't know—hotel, I suppose." I said, "Well, if you'd like to come and spend Christmas with us, we'd love to have you." He said, "Oh yes, please, that would be wonderful. We've had enough of the hotel." So he and his wife and two children drove over to our house about midday, and we had turkey around three in the afternoon. Bonnie's family was with us, and because her grandmother was a teetotaler I had to serve drinks in the laundry room. Bill carved the turkey, and after dinner they put the children to sleep in our bed. Unfortunately, the children promptly wet the bed.

At about 7 o'clock Bill said it would be nice to go up to Philip and Jack's and have a look at their place, so we called them up and they said, "All right, come along." We had some other guests with us, and Oliver said, "I'll drive ahead and show you the way." It isn't easy up in the hills unless you know them, and it was a terribly stormy night. They all set off and they came back quite late, so I said to Oliver, "What happened? How did everyone get up there?" On the way up, one of the roads had washed out and there was a flare to warn people. Bill drove straight into it, as only he would. Oliver carried one child up a steep hill, Bill carried the other, and

Alice just walked up as best she could. Philip and Jack told me next day that the first thing they asked was, "May we put the children in your beds?" Philip and Jack said, "Yes, of course," and the children promptly wet their beds. So this very saturated two weeks fulfilled itself in every way, including the next morning for me. When I went into the kitchen to turn on the coffee maker, I discovered that the bottom had fallen out of the water heater, so we were flooded out. There was only one thing to do; I cried with laughter. There was no point in doing anything else, and that is the story of the recording of the quintets.

PRO ARTE QUARTET

We admired the Pro Arte Quartet very much. When we had only just started to play, we would go and hear them, and we became extremly enamored with them. It was because of them that we became a quartet. They were very good colleagues and good friends. Philip and I did the sextets with them on one occasion and there was no time to rehearse. We met in the artists' room before doing the Brahms B♭, and they simply told us, "We do this here, and we do this there," and we went out and played. I believe they often worked like this. One evening after we'd played with them at the Chelsea Music Club, they said they were recording Schubert the next day, and it was one they had never played before.

LAURI KENNEDY

Lauri Kennedy was a wonderful cellist if ever there was one. He had a sound that lifted and exalted one. You could often hear him playing as first cello with the BBC Orchestra, which was interesting. [Arturo] Toscanini had demanded that they have Lauri Kennedy, and Lauri was offered the job, but he had never played in an orchestra before. He had a wonderful nerve. The last time I saw Lauri Kennedy I was sitting on a plane in Sydney, Australia, waiting to take a flight to Melbourne. There was an empty seat next to me, and at the last minute a man jostled into it, and it turned out to be Lauri Kennedy. We got right down to talking, and he had a wonderful sense of humor. He was staying at the same hotel in Melbourne that we were, and we continued to talk and drink in the hotel room. We'd left the cello on the bed, and he kept picking it up and playing. As he did the famous Rondo from Boccherini's quintet, he repeated, "No wrists; you mustn't use your wrists in cello playing—not at all, no wrist." I've thought about this over the years, and he had a point.

YEHUDI AND HEPHZIBAH MENUHIN

One of the nicest musicians I have known is Yehudi Menuhin. He is always so sensitive, always concerned about other people. "Are you comfortable? Are you all right? Is that what you would like, or is there something you would rather have?"

I remember Yehudi playing the Elgar; I believe it was the first time he came to England, and he was 13 years old. He came on in little gray shorts and socks and a tennis shirt buttoned at the neck. This was in Albert Hall, with about 10,000 people. The Elgar is about an hour long; then there was an intermission, and then he played Brahms. That's an endurance feat that a mature person would find difficult, but even at 13, Yehudi seemed to be a mature artist of 60 years. When he was rehearsing with Elgar, he played a particular passage of octaves, and then he asked, "Why did you write octaves?" Elgar said, "Because I wanted more sound." Yehudi said, "Didn't you know, Sir Edward, that you get less sound if you play octaves than if you play a single line?" Of course he was right, but he was such a charmer. I will never forget the huge, rich sound he had. It filled the Albert Hall.

We had some wonderful times with Yehudi. He bought a large piece of land on a mountain about 40 miles south of Berkeley, where he would go in the summer for his vacation. We used to go down and play with him, and it was always wonderful. We'd have lunch with him, spend the afternoon playing, have dinner, and then come home. This was a man who, at the age of ten, played the Beethoven Concerto with Fritz Busch in Carnegie Hall, where police were positioned throughout the hall to stop people who wanted to touch him. At his summer place, there was a guard box at the entrance to the road going up his mountain. When visitors arrived, the guard would phone up to the house and say, "Is it all right to admit these people?" And Yehudi would say yea or nay.

On one of these visits we were playing the A-Major Mozart with him and we came to the slow variations with the cello ostinato in the coda. I played a few measures of this, and he turned to me and said, "Are you making that up?" I said, "No, I wish I could." Of course, when you play it all the way through, it does make sense.

We did one or two concerts at his house, and I remember one in which we played the Brahms C-Minor Piano Quartet with Adolph Baller, a very fine pianist. Yehudi was bothered with his bow at this time and unfortunately there had been much talk about it. When I came to a slow movement, he would turn around and watch my bowing. You could tell it worried him, and he was very honest about it. He told us he had never been taught how to use his fingers on the bow. People would say, "Do it this way," and he would do it, and then one day he thought, "How do I do it? What am I doing to make this happen?" and that was his undoing. While it had

Yehudi Menuhin
and his wife at
their home in
Los Gatos, California

been subconscious, it was fine, but when it was brought into conscious-
ness, it was the end in a way. He also told us that if he were alone in a
room with his father for five minutes, he would be drenched, and his sister, Hephzibah, wouldn't come back home while their father was alive, so
I think his father must have been something of an ogre.

Hephzibah was a great pianist and an outrageous person. She was auda-
cious but nevertheless exuded charm. We did a tour with her in New
Zealand for about ten weeks and had a fabulous time (though it was bitterly cold weather on the south island). We did a lot of rehearsing with
Hephzibah, who is a wonderful person to play with, a born chamber music
player. I do not think most pianists are; they are trained to play big concertos, to make a big noise. Often they're trained to play on their own without
any warmth or consideration for other players, so I do not think many of
them can play chamber music. Myra Hess can, and certainly Hephzibah
can. She was great fun. I still have a book of limericks that she and her
companion at the time, Clarice, wrote about us.

Hephzibah was about four feet high and when she went out on the
platform, the audience only had to see her face and they were captivated.
I have never seen anything like this. We did a lot of concerts with her and
also some partying. On our tour she had to go back to Auckland to play
a concerto with the symphony there, and we went on down to Dunedin,
where she was going to join us. Before she got there, we went down to the
shops and bought her a hat—a terrible sort of Victorian hat—and various
other toys for her. We knew from Clarice that she wore as her underclothes
what she called her "loose covers," which were her husband's underwear.
Apparently she used to get in the tub at night and wash them out, so we
bought her a tugboat to take in her bath. We also got her a copy of a piece
by [Cécile] Chaminade in which we wrote our own directions, including
at the end "kindly wash hands after each use." I got a key from the manager for her bedroom (which happened to be next to mine), and we
arranged everything, including artificial flowers, and it was quite a show.

I heard her come in, and there were shrieks of laughter from Clarice.
Then I heard the telephone ring—some young reporter had come to inter-
view her. I heard her being very serious with him, and then she said, "Now,
wait a minute." Then she came and got me and absolutely seriously said,
"Look at these wonderful presents that my wonderful friends the Grillers
have given me. Aren't they generous?" She went on like this, and the
reporter never saw through it, so it all came out in the papers the next day.

After that we played for a few days in Christchurch, New Zealand.
Before one of the concerts Hephzibah was ironing her dress, which had to
be done in the passage outside her bedroom. I wandered out and started
talking to her, and we were in the midst of a conversation when a woman
came down the passage and said, "Excuse me, may I go through?"

Hephzibah replied, "Indeed you may not. Can't you see we're having a committee meeting?" The woman said, "Really, I'm so sorry. Excuse me," and she went back to her room. We didn't see her again.

One morning at rehearsal, Hephzibah said, "I'm tired of going out after the concert. Why don't we get some food and eat in the hotel?" We thought this was a good idea, so she asked Clarice to pick up something for us. We met Clarice after we had finished rehearsing, and she was laughing her head off. Hephzibah said, "What did you get for tonight?" and Clarice said, "Among other things, I got a mutton bird." Hephzibah said, "A mutton bird, for God's sake, a mutton bird?" It seems that this is a bird that nests on the ground in Tasmania, and it lives on fish. It's supposed to be quite good eating, but you have to boil it for two days to get rid of the fish before you can even think of eating it. You have to remember that we were going to have this little party in Hephzibah's room because she was the only person in the hotel with a fireplace, and it was cold, and now we had this mutton bird to cook. I was in charge of the mutton bird, and I was cooking it on a little coal shovel that we used to put coal on the fire.

The Grillers in public rehearsal, summer school in Wellington, New Zealand

I had taken off my jacket and white waistcoat, and I was in my pants, and unbeknownst to me, all the grease from the mutton bird was running down the handle and onto my trouser leg. What a mess! And the mutton bird never did get cooked. We had to throw it out, and we had our supper of cheese and cold meat and salad. While this was being prepared, I got a hunk of garlic and stuffed it in Hephzibah's bed. The next morning the inevitable cup of tea came in at 7 o'clock, and the maid said

Colin with Yehudi Menuhin, a student, and violinist Zaven Melikian

apologetically, "Oh, Miss Menuhin has asked me to give you this." She handed me the little Victorian hat we had bought, and it was full of salad and the remains of the party. They had dressed it up to look like a beautiful bouquet, and Hephzibah had given the maid ten shillings to give it to us.

Hephzibah was a wonderful pianist. No one else we played with was so much fun—even Edwin Fischer, who was rather a soloist and also a magnificent pianist. After we had our first rehearsal with him, Sidney said, "Let's arrange other rehearsals," and he said, "What on earth for? I'm going to play differently every time we sit down to play together. There is no point in rehearsing." He always traveled with his old nanny, and he was absolutely scared stiff of the ocean. He got up his courage to travel from Germany to England, but he wouldn't go to America. The thought of all that ocean was too much for him. I heard a wonderful story about one of his recitals at Queen's Hall. He finished the program with Op. 111 of Beethoven, and he botched up part of it; he played a mass of wrong notes. He turned to the audience and threw up his hands. Then he started again and played it magnificently. It's nice to see this breaking away from the norm of the well-mannered concert. I have always thought it a good idea to have a bit of conversation between artists and audiences to break the ice.

When we were in Christchurch, Hephzibah told us that once she and Yehudi had given a recital and he had not played very well. When he came out, the people were trying to touch him; they were full of adoration. He waved to them, and he said to Hephzibah, "Poor dears, I wish I had played better for them." It must have been a very big heartache for him.

He was down here not too long ago, and I talked to him after a rehearsal. He was very subdued—and very much a gentleman, as he always was—but the music making during his rehearsal was quite wonderful. It seemed to be coming from another world. His eyes seem to see so much more than is in this world, so much more than is on the printed page.

Ernest Bloch rehearsing
his Third Quartet (written
for the Grillers) with
the Griller Quartet

Composers,
Critics, and Allies

3

WE MET SIR ARTHUR BLISS BECAUSE he wanted some bowings and fingerings for his "music for strings." He called to ask if we would do it for him, and of course we were happy to. I have always liked his music, which is fresh and alive, and he made good use of major and minor almost simultaneously. He came to our house in Hampstead, which had a dumbwaiter in the kitchen—a lift that carried food and came up through the floor. When it was down, the floor dropped back into place, but it was always a little risky. We warned Arthur not to tread on it, but he was quite an excitable man, and sure enough, in his excitement he stepped right on it. He caught himself by his elbow, so he didn't fall down into the kitchen, luckily, but he didn't stop talking for one second.

Over time we got to know Arthur, who was a lovely man, and he wrote his last string quartet for us. He was very proud of this piece because it was difficult, but I think it's a very nice quartet. We played it first in the Edinburgh Festival. We were getting the movements here in California as he wrote them, and the last one came just before we left for England, so we learned it on the ship going over.

We used to do a festival on the Isle of Wight at J.B. Priestley's house, where we would stay for a week. Bliss was frequently there as well. There was a huge ship's bell in the fireplace in the living room, which Bliss would hit to give us an A, and that's what we would tune to. Once when we were playing around, I became aware of a shaggy dog at my side; it was Bliss under a rug on his hands and knees! Just after Sidney bought his house in Kensington, he suspected he had dry rot. We were in a taxi with Bliss when Sidney was telling us this, and Bliss said, "Sidney, all the dry rot in London emanates from my house."

ARNOLD BAX

Arnold Bax came into our lives early on. We learned his first quartet, and our friendship grew from there. We have played, many times, a wonderful piano quintet of his, and I wish we could get a copy, because I don't think the piece has been played out here. It should be; it's quite powerful and emotional.

I have always been grateful for the first quartet Arnold Bax wrote. When we first came to America, we borrowed 800 pounds to get here and to give a recital in New York. This was the only entry into America at the time. We decided to open with Bax's quartet, because people here wouldn't know it, and we did know it very well. After that we would play the Mozart C Major and finish with Beethoven's Op. 95. When we landed in New York, Myra Hess (God bless her) put off the work for a week to give us a chance to get used to New York. We went to the managers at NBC, and they said very firmly, "We are only managing this concert. We are not your managers." We did the concert, beginning with the Bax. At the end of the slow movement, to our astonishment, people stood up and cheered. After the Mozart, we discovered that our manager had been around to every critic to find out what they thought, and during the intermission, we signed a contract.

When Bax first wrote his quartet for us, he used a rhythm in the last movement that was reminiscent of Chopin. Harriet Cohen, his pianist, said to him, "You can't possibly do that, Arnold," and he was stumped. Finally I suggested that he change the meter, which he did, and that was how it was printed. Actually, something similar happened with Bliss. When we did the slow movement of his quartet before playing in Edinburgh, at one of the rehearsals I said to him, "You know, this is none of my business, but these two measures should be 3/4 rather than 4/4." He thought about it and said, "You're absolutely right," so they were published that way.

CYRIL SCOTT AND PERCY GRAINGER

With Cyril Scott we had a rather strange and difficult relationship. Cyril called us up and asked if we would play his quartet for a few friends. We said yes, we would, so he sent us a score and told us his friends would be here in about a week. Could we have it ready by then? We made a date to do it before we saw the music, which was safe except for the Scherzo, which was extremely difficult. It had a moving beat in eighth notes—5/8, 1/8, 9/8, 2/8, no/8, 12/8, and so on. This was bad enough, but unfortunatly the other parts never quite tallied; one would have a 7/8 and another would have an 8/8, and so on throughout the piece. We were up until 2 in the morning trying to work it out. We did work it out in a way: we rewrote the whole thing in 4/4 with cross accents, and pasted it above his manuscript so he could take it off afterward.

The first person to arrive for the concert was Percy Grainger, who was a very nice man. "Well," he said, "what's this piece like?" We said, "Oh, it's a very good quartet," and then we mentioned the difficulty of the Scherzo. One of us said rather timidly, "Well, actually, if he had written it in 4/4 with cross accents, it would have been the same thing." He replied, "Absolutely not. It wouldn't have made any sense." So we didn't say any more. The other guests arrived and someone asked, "What tempo do you want?" Grainger said, "Does it have any metronome marking?" We replied that it did, and he proceeded to take a piece of string with a weight on it from his pocket. He

stood up on a chair swinging it and said, "This is your tempo." We played in that tempo, and when we came to the Scherzo, we played in 4/4 with cross accents. The moment it was over, Grainger jumped up and said, "You see, that made absolute sense. If you'd played it in 4/4 with cross accents, it wouldn't have done." We never said a word, of course.

Sir Arthur Bliss, Master of the Queen's Music

DARIUS MILHAUD

AND IGOR STRAVINSKY

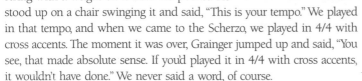

Darius Milhaud (incidentally, it's pronounced *milo;* in the part of France he and his wife came from, the *l* is pronounced) wrote a viola quintet that we commissioned. It was far too busy and too clever to ever be a successful piece. That was one of Milhaud's problems when he wrote in this delightful French style. His technique was so incredible that he just couldn't help himself. We spent some time at the Santa Barbara music academy one year when he was there. He would sit and talk to people and compose at the same time.

Howard Bliss and Stravinsky were at the festival as well, and one night they gave a dinner party at the Santa Barbara country club. We were there as a quartet, the Milhauds were there, the conductor Hans Lett was there, and of course the Stravinskys were there. At one point I looked around the table and everyone was talking about himself. I was sitting next to Sidney, who was doing nothing but telling rude limericks all evening.

Gregor Piatigorsky at the California Cello Club, circa 1956; Margaret Rowell, cofounder of the club with Colin, is seen in the center, behind Piatigorsky

At about this time we began a rather strange relationship with Stravinsky. Not too long after the dinner party we wanted to commission a quartet from him. We were in New York at the time and we knew he was there as well and that he always stayed at the Pierot Hotel. My colleagues didn't have the guts to call him up, so I said, "OK, I'll call him." I had expected to face a battery of secretaries, but he answered the phone hi self, to my astonishment. I said, "This is Colin Hampton. I'm the cellist in the Griller Quartet—you won't remember me," and he replied, "Oh yes I do, Griller Quartet." I asked what was the chance of commissioning a quartet, and he said, "Ugh, my dear, I am so busy; I am two years behind." So we didn't get the quartet from him.

We met him again three years later in Cuba. We were playing there, and he was conducting there, and I went up to him and said, "Hello, Mr. Stravinsky. How are you? You won't remember me," and he said, "Yes, you're Colin Hampton of the Griller Quartet." And the same thing happened again later when we were crossing the Atlantic. He was traveling incognito, so we hadn't bothered him. One day he had been down to the ship's shop and he was trying to make his way back to his cabin with a package. It was somewhat rough, so I went over to him and said, "Mr. Stravinsky, can I help you?" And he said, "Yes, please, if you would, I would be grateful. You're Colin Hampton of the Griller Quartet, aren't you?" It was extraordinary to me that he remembered. He was a lovely man.

Some artists are very easy to work with. Arnold Bax is not at all fussy about the performance of his music. He said once to Sidney and me, "Play any note you want: it doesn't matter." Of course we didn't, but he certainly had a free spirit. Milhaud was also fairly easily pleased. One night we played his first quartet, which consisted of four movements, and two or three days later we played it again at a series of concerts in San Francisco. He was not sure about the third movement, and I think he was right; it was possibly a pretentious movement. He told us in Berkeley's Wheeler Hall, "When you play it here, play all four movements, and when you play it in San Francisco, play three; leave that slow movement out." We did, and afterward he said, "All right, in the future, just leave that movement out. Never play it again—it's bad." When we played it in public, the critics took us to task for leaving it out. If critics asked, "Why did you leave it out?" we said, "Well, this is the request of Milhaud." They would reply, "A composer has no right, once he has published a work, to change it" (which I think is a lot of baloney, but I suppose I think critics are nearly always wrong).

ARNOLD SCHOENBERG

When we were doing the summer school with Arnold Schoenberg, one night after dinner, all the kids were in the common room, and someone put on a phonograph record of the third act of *Die Meistersinger*. Within seconds Schoenberg was weeping, and he wept all the way through. Aterward I said to him, "Arnold, you write the type of music you write, and yet obviously you're quite moved by Wagner," and he told me, "When I was a young man I was too close to Wagner. It was too strong, so I had to invent my system to get away from it."

One night that same summer we put on some of the Schoenberg quartets. Toward the end of this long and tedious quartet, suddenly a simple little German folk song appeared. I asked Arnold, "Why did you include that?" He said, "Well, it seemed right." So he must have had his reasons, though I couldn't say what they were.

One of the biggest phenomena in my time was Toscanini. England, for one, certainly went crazy for him—so much so that he was an absolute pest as far as I was concerned. First and foremost, I did not like his conducting. I have to give him credit for the fact that he got an incredible clarity out of the orchestra. But it was absolutely without humanity, even rigid. If Toscanini had been in one hall and [Sir Thomas] Beecham in another, I would have gone to see Beecham any day. Toscanini seemed to have a power over people and could do no wrong. On one occasion he snatched the camera from a journalist, threw it to the ground, and stamped on it!

However, it was more than one's life was worth to criticize Toscanini or to say you didn't like him. You would have had to defend yourself to a degree that I didn't feel like doing. One summer I was doing a summer school in Santa Barbara, California, with Schoenberg. One day I gathered my courage and asked him, "Arnold, what do you think of Toscanini?" And he spat and said, "That bandmaster," with a great deal of derision in his voice. He went on to tell me that Toscanini had received all his musical training in military school, which explained everything.

Ernest Bloch

ERNEST BLOCH

Perhaps the greatest person it was my luck to meet was Ernest Bloch. We met in 1938. We had already learned Bloch's Piano Quintet, his string quartet (there was only one at that time), and the [Circus] Pieces. String Quartet No. 1 is to me one of the great works in the world. It was a logical conclusion, as far as I am concerned, to the Beethoven quartets. I would put Bloch in front of Schubert and Brahms anytime. There was a Bloch Society in London in 1938 that presented a festival of Bloch's music. Whatever Bloch had written was played, and I remember we played the quintet with [pianist] Louis Kentner. Bloch came over from Switzerland for the festival. He returned right afterward, and we weren't to meet again until 1946, after the war was over, in San Francisco.

Shortly after the festival, we received a manuscript from him that said *Deux Morceaux*, but there was only one. We were very excited that he had written it and dedicated it to us, and we immediately started to learn it. About a month later we got a frantic cable from him saying, "Whatever you do, don't play it. Letter following." He had decided he was going to write some of the material in the second quartet in a bigger piece, and so we never did play it. In the meantime war broke out, and when the second quartet arrived it had been sent from America, where Bloch was now living. He sent this quartet, and we copied our parts and we played it. We premiered it in London during the war and played it several places. It got a tremendous review from Ernest Newman, who had sent for the score before we played it. He studied it for about a month, so he really knew what he was listening to.

Before the war we played the first quartet, and throughout the war we played the second. After the war we found ourselves touring Germany, and then we returned to the States in 1946 and did a big tour. After playing in Los Angeles, we came up to San Francisco for four days, and Bloch came down from Agate Beach, Oregon. We all stayed in a hotel on Market Street and resumed our friendship in this way. After we had talked for several hours, Sidney said, "Well, would you like to hear some of your second quartet?" Bloch said, "Yes, of course I would." Since we were in the hotel, we played the first and third movements, the slow, quiet ones. He left the room without a word, and we thought, "My God, what have we done? We must have made a botched reading of it. We got hold of the wrong end of the stick."

The next day we went over to the music department at Berkeley, where we were due to play for the faculty. A critic for the newspaper was also there. This time we played all the way through. Afterward Bloch came over and kissed us all in turn and said, "You see, when you played it yesterday, it didn't make any sense to me without the other two movements." At his request we played it two or three times, and I ended up with a bleeding finger and blood all over my cello. I always did anyway with that piece because all of the pizzicati in the last movement.

Just shortly before this time, we were engaged to play at the Music Academy of the West, and Bloch had a birthday while he was there. He was living in one of the master's houses by himself, and Ada Clement, his good friend from the San Francisco Conservatory of Music, said to us, "I think July 24 is his birthday. Why don't you get up and play that piece he sent you?" So we did. We got up and went over to his house at seven in the morning, a lovely sunny morning. We took our stands over, no chairs, propped ourselves up outside his house, and played. There was dead silence for about five minutes, and then he came storming out. "Who has been writing my music?" He was furious until we showed him the manuscript in his own hand, and then he was delighted. He'd forgotten all about it. We had to play it several times for him. He later did write a second piece, which is published now, and so the *Deux Morceaux* became two pieces.

During those two months in Santa Barbara we played the second quartet quite a lot, and then one night in the common room he asked if we would play No. 1. We said, "Look, we haven't played it for some time. It's going to be rusty." He said, "That's all right; just play it." So we did. When we had finished, he got up and with a sort of crush on his heart he said, "Why can't I write that sort of music now?" It was a heartbreaking cry.

I remember talking to Bloch on one occasion in Santa Barbara. He and I were alone, and we got on the subject of Beethoven quartets. He commented that Op. 59, No. 1, was a giant of a piece and that Op. 95 is a mouse. Then he followed this up by saying, "But, Mighty Mouse."

It was interesting to hear Bloch lecture, and he gave quite a few lectures during that summer school. He would take the flesh off the skeleton, so to speak, and show you the skeleton, but then he would put the flesh back. Curiously enough, Schoenberg did the same thing, but he never put the flesh back. You were just left with a note or a stroke to a note. So it was interesting to see the difference between these two.

Bloch looked like a man of granite. His face seemed hewn out of rock. He would yell, sing, shriek; he was always in a terrible state of excitement. He was only about five feet tall, but he was sheer granite, and yet he also had incredible charm. The first performance I heard of the Violin Concerto was when he played it in his hotel suite for us. He was a very fine violinist. He had been a pupil of Ysaÿe, but he hadn't played the violin for about 20 years. When he wanted to write a concerto, he took out his violin and practiced for about three months. He could do tenths and octaves with a very passable technique, but it was curious to see this man of granite standing up there playing with a very sweet French sound, which he must have gotten from Ysaÿe. Nevertheless it was quite wonderful. He also played us one of his symphonies on the piano. Bloch was to write three more quartets, which we premiered, so altogether we premiered four out of five.

During that time in Santa Barbara I was feeling very badly about Zara Nelsova, that she had not really made the headlines that she should have done. I felt this was a great injustice, and I said to Ernest while we were there, "Can't she come and study cello works with you?" He said, "Yes, of course she can. She can come and stay with Margaret [his wife] and the six cats." So I wrote to Zara and told her that she should do this, and she wrote back, "If there are cats I can't possibly go." I wrote to her again and said, "Cats or no cats, you're bloody well going!" And go she did. Because of this, of course, she got to record *Schelomo* with Bloch, and he wrote his three unaccompanied cello suites and dedicated them to her. I felt strongly that Zara should be recording, so I asked London FFRR to take

her on, and finally they did. She said she didn't think it was worth doing, but I told her, "If you get nothing, do it. What a way of becoming known." So she did.

The Grillers playing Bloch's *Deux Morceaux* outside his window for his birthday

The woman who was running the summer school at Santa Barbara Music Academy of the West was not terribly bright—a little thick, as the British would say. One night everybody was in the common room, as was the habit after dinner. She began to talk and she happened to say something rather disrespectful about European musicians, where upon Bloch lit into her in no uncertain terms. It was a tremendous diatribe and he finished by saying, "In any case, what are you Americans except 36 feet of bowels with a hole at each end?" I've never seen a room empty so fast.

Bloch lived at Agate Beach in Oregon, and we used to go up and stay for a week or so. We worked through all the quartets, and these were wonderfully rewarding days. Bloch had a beautiful house, and his studio was over his garage. He was there by himself, with no telephone, and he had a staircase right down onto the beach. He would go for walks there and pick up agates. The maid had given him an electric polishing machine, so he had hundreds and hundreds of polished agates. He gave us quite a few, and it's always been my habit that when someone has learned a major Bloch piece, I give them one of these polished agates. I have only three or four left now.

Ernest Bloch with the
Grillers, Santa Barbara
Mission, 1947

Each of Bloch's string quartets won the Critics' Prize in New York for the best work of the year. In the last one he used the 12-tone system, just to see if it could be done, but no one ever spotted it, which was really a tour de force, I think. He didn't approve of fashions in music, and he made a remark once that the "isms" of today (cubism and so forth) would be the "wasms" of tomorrow.

I talked with Bloch one night up at his son's house in Portland about *Schelomo,* because I felt that so much nonsense had been said about the piece. He complained bitterly about everybody playing it too slowly. In fact, on one occasion we were in New York with him when *Schelomo* was being played by the first cello of the Boston Symphony. Bloch took out his pocket watch at the beginning of the piece and stuck it on his knee. He was furious because it was about five minutes too long, and five minutes on a 23-minute piece is quite a lot. He had a horror of people playing his music too slowly, and this was one occasion where it showed. I asked Bloch that night at Ivan's house about *Schelomo,* "Isn't your metronome mark rather fast at the beginning?" He said, "Well, 66 or thereabouts." It's interesting to me that everybody plays *Schelomo* too slowly, and I do think Bloch's metronome mark is too fast, but I have come to the conclusion that most of the cellists who play just do not possess a score or have not bothered to read it. In the cello part there is no metronome mark and everything is in Italian, and in the piano part there is no metronome mark, and everything is in French. The score has the metronome marks, and they are there for anybody to see, so how people can continue to make this misreading, I don't know. This is a piece I like to teach, because I had the good fortune to work with Bloch and to know what he wants. I trust my good fortune, and I like to pass it on wherever I can.

FRIENDS AND SUPPORTERS

We met Mrs. [Elizabeth] Sprague Coolidge the first time we played in Boston in about 1939 or early 1940. There had been a tremendous snowstorm, and people were stranded all over the city. The mayor was in prison because he had sold all the snow ploughs, and there were several feet of snow in the streets. We needed to get from our hotel to Jordan Hall (which, by the way, was one of the finest halls I have ever played in). We walked since no taxis were available, and I carried my cello on my head. There were six people in the hall, and our rule was that if there was one more person in the auditorium than sitting on the platform, we would play, and so we did. The six people were the Coolidge family, and we became good friends. Mrs. Coolidge did her best to persuade us not to go back to England, to stay in the United States. Every time we went to Boston we had dinner with her in her hotel in Cambridge. One night she had another quartet there and we all trouped in to dinner. I was sitting on her left, and she turned to me after hearing all the musicians' talk and said, "No rose without a thorn, and no quartet without a viola player."

Mrs. Steinway was another wonderful woman. She lived in a lovely apartment on Park Avenue in New York, but there was nothing swank about her. There was a very nice meeting between Leonard Bernstein and Mrs. Steinway. When they were introduced, she said, "Well, it's very nice to finally meet you, Mr. Bernstein," and he said, "No, excuse me, the name is Bern*steen*." She replied, "In that case, you'd better call me Mrs. *Steen*way."

Edith and Sir Osbert Sitwell were also very interesting people. I dreaded the day their brother got knighted Sir Sacheverell. What a mouthful! It was a family knighthood that was handed down. They had a beautiful house in London, in Chelsea. I remember a wonderful Holbein picture in the hallway downstairs and some beautiful glass— it was almost like a museum. We used to go up to their castle in Derbyshire. It was a huge country house, one of these 200- or 300-room affairs, but they lived in just

two or three rooms and had a butler, and that was it. The family had been very wealthy at one time and they had also had a castle in Italy. But the father had been pro-Mussolini and he had given his money, castle, and belongings to support Mussolini, which unfortunately impoverished the family. We used to go and play for Edith and Sir Osbert, and they were always very sweet and nice.

I was grateful to the Sitwells for the good things they did. They were an enormous help to Willie Walton and to Dylan Thomas. I had four or five books from Edith and a few from Osbert, and the ones from Edith are inscribed something like "To Colin; thank you for a wonderful experience last night," rather a dubious inscription! Edith was quite a gossip, and she looked rather like a witch with her long talons, long face, and long, heavy body. She liked to shock, and she came from an era in which it was good to be shocking. Lady Adalina Morall also did that sort of thing, and she was known as Lady Utterly Immoral.

Augustus John is another person who comes to mind. There was a command performance, and we were to go to Buckingham Palace to play for the Queen Mother (still queen at the time) while she was having her portrait painted. We had not been back long from our six months' stay in the United States when we were summoned. We arrived at the palace and were being shown down a long corridor in which there were a remarkable number of windows. Each window recess contained a small marble pillar that obviously had held a bust. All the valuables had been taken out and buried somewhere for the duration of the war, so there was nothing on these little pillars, except one, which held a packet of All Bran!

John was painting and smoking as hard as he could the whole time, and we were playing in a little anteroom with the doors open. The queen had more or less expressed what she wished to hear. At one point she said, "Sir John, would you mind if I had a rest?" He allowed her to get down, and she came into the little anteroom and spoke to us. We had been told to call her first "Your Majesty" and after that "ma'am," but we never called her anything. She put us very much at our ease. She knew where we had been, all the places we had toured in America, so she must have studied very hard. She was absolutely charming and vivacious, with the wonderful ability to make you feel comfortable. We asked afterward if we could keep the check and frame it, but we were not allowed to do so.

I also want to mention Howard Ferguson, a composer who was a contemporary of ours. Howard lived in London after the war, and I lived in the country, and every so often he would call me up and say, "I say, old thing, do you think I could come and stay with you for a week?" When the air raids became too much, he would feel he needed to get away to get a little sleep. I was about 30 miles out of London, so it was a little quieter. One Sunday night when Howard was there, I had to leave for camp at 5 o'clock the next morning, and he said, "Bring me a cup of coffee before you go." The next morning I took the coffee up, and I said, "Howard, it's absolutely pouring rain. You won't want to go for a long walk in the country today." He said, "Oh yes, I shall!" I lived near the Icknield Way [an ancient trail, much improved by the Romans], where Shakespeare used to walk when he went to London, and Howard said, "Every so often I have to take ground that has been trodden by people 2,000 years before me. I just get something out of the soil." This is a remark I have never forgotten, and I think it explains a great deal of English music—why it is as alive today as it was 2,000 years ago.

ALEX COWAN

Alex Cowan was a very unfortunate man in many respects. He was a not-very-competent violinist who lived in his imagination most of the time, unaware of what was going on around him. And yet this man had an insight into music. Of all the people I met, Alex's insight was perhaps the greatest. He wasn't the easiest of men to work with. He was adamant in his judgments. But he was usually right, and he saw so strongly, as Ernest Newman said, the "back of the note" and what it meant, what its

significance was. This is the terrible thing about talking about music—
you can't! But Alex showed me more of what music was about than
anybody else, and I'm deeply grateful to him for this. He also made
me realize how much a performance misses what's on the printed page,
and it staggers me to this day. There is so much in front of us that, if
we read it very carefully, is a wonderful guide. Usually we take no
notice. We come across a bunch of eighth or 16th notes, and we play
them spiccato without observing whether or not there are dots on the
notes or considering what the implication of the music is. This goes
for Beethoven, Brahms, Mozart, and all the classics. I grant you there
are times you have to make up your own mind, because editors are
notoriously bad.

AMATEURS

I believe the subject of amateurs is worth some consideration. First and
foremost, I think we owe our thanks to amateurs of the past 100 or so
years. It's because of them that many wonderful Italian instruments and
bows and French bows have been preserved to this day. It's been my
experience that professionals made us use them as a means to the end,
and they don't love them in the same way that amateurs do. Amateurs are
the ones who have taken such care of them, and I carry them around in
my heart for that.

A curious aspect of amateurs is that there is a very defined pecking
order. There is more snobbishness among the amateurs, in fact, than
among professionals. But there is also a wonderful spirit of professionalism
in amateurs. For example, they know the opus numbers. They will say,
we played 81 or 92 or 312, and they expect you to know what it is. I
must confess I have never been able to remember Köchel numbers and
most opus numbers. I do know the Beethoven quartets, but that's about
it. One day in a series of lectures Schoenberg said, "What would you
like me to lecture about next week?" I said, "Op. 127," and he said, "Don't
give me the telephone numbers!" I said, "I only gave you the telephone
number because there happened to be two in E♭." So he didn't know his
opus numbers either. But amateurs, no matter how miserably they play, all
talk about their opus numbers. Amateurs certainly are a bunch to be reck-
oned with. One I knew was so keen on playing that he played at his own
wedding. He could go one better and play at his own funeral.

Some years ago the dean of the law school invited us (the quartet) and
Honor to dinner. He also invited a man who was a psychiatrist and his
wife. It started off rather badly. When we were introduced to this couple,
she said, "Oh, tell me, do you feel nervous when you walk out onto the

platform?" I said, "Yes, I suppose most artists do." She replied, "Oh, you must be a very insecure person. You'd better come and see my husband; he'll cure you." Then as we went into dinner, this little man was holding forth just as we were sitting down. He said, "Now this man Bloch! Of course he doesn't mean a note he writes; it's all done with his tongue in his cheek," which infuriated me. I turned to my hostess and said, "May I?" and she said, "Go to it." So I said to him, "How dare you say such a thing about a sincere artist, you who know nothing about music. You ought to be ashamed of yourself." I don't think I'd been so rude to anybody in public in my life, but I wasn't going to take that nonsense. The evening got worse as it went on. After dinner our hostess said something to the psychiatrist about not liking to drive in San Francisco, because she was nervous about the steep hills, and he said, "Oh, you and I will take a little walk in the garden, and I'll soon cure you of your fears." As they went out, her husband yelled, "That's right, frighten her out of her fear!"

Colin with Isolda on her last trip to California

CRITICS

Generally I think critics are absolutely pernicious and useless. They don't do any good, they do a great deal of harm, they hold jobs they shouldn't have, and usually they are ignorant. I've always marveled that young critics will go to a concert to hear a brand-new work, and they will criticize it from start to finish after one hearing. Are they such geniuses? Come on!

Many years ago, we did a performance of Szymanowski's quartet in which he had drawn straight lines between notes. As you know, that indicates a glissando, and there were quite a lot in this piece. The next day we got hauled over the coals for our excessive sliding. Of course you can say nothing; you just have to take it and sit quietly. I always remember J.B. Priestley talking about "the boys," meaning the critics, in a very sarcastic voice. I also remember the wonderful occasion when Bliss was about to do his opera *The Olympians*, and a critic called him up and said, "I would very much like to see the score of your opera." Bliss knew very well that what he really wanted was to talk to Bliss about it and have Bliss tell him all about it. But Bliss was much too wily a bird for that. He had the score sitting on the piano, and he said, "Now, Mr. So-and-So, I'm afraid I have to go out, but I'm honoring your request. There is the score, there is the keyboard, and the house will be all yours. Enjoy yourself." Then he left, which is not what the young fellow had intended at all.

On another wonderful occasion, the great critic Ernest Newman put everything in its right place. This was shortly after the war, and there had just been a performance of Strauss—I believe it was *Salome*. The day after, some young critics said, "Ah, what a wonderful performance, the greatest *Salome* we've ever heard." As Newman pointed out, it was, in fact, the only *Salome* they'd ever heard.

In the 30-odd years of our quartet, only twice did critics write to us before we produced a new work and ask for the score. One was Ernest Newman, on the first of Bloch's quartets in London, and the other one was Olin Downes in New York, who made the same request before we produced a Bloch quartet. So these two men had a chance to look at the score to try to understand what the composer was trying to do instead of damning it or praising it out of hand without knowing what the music was about.

One time Casals produced a *St. Matthew Passion* in New York, and I went because I was going up to Vermont anyway to the Marlboro Festival. For Casals' performance, the New York critic Schonberg came out. He said what a wonderful innovation Casals had made by splitting the boys' chorus, one part on each side of the stage, which is exactly what Bach had indicated in the score. A few days later at Marlboro, Schonberg came up to me and asked, now that the Griller Quartet had finished playing, what was I going to do with myself. I said straight out, "Tell people like you what I think of you," and he then disappeared. I do not see that critics add value to anything. The work is written, and they cannot take it away. They have only their feeble opinion, which can be as wrong as mine. And I think they play with people's opinions, which is a great pity.

Colin at about age 21

Thoughts on Technique

CELLISTS ARE A WONDERFUL BREED. In the whole of my life I have met only two cellists I couldn't get on with—only two. I think this speaks extremely well for any group of musicians playing the same instrument. Surely it must be something in the instrument itself that attracts a certain type of person. During the war when cellists would see each other practicing, one might say, "Hey, what finger do you do that with? What bowing? How do you manage that?" And the person playing would always explain it. But if you saw a violinist practicing a Brahms concerto and another violinist came anywhere near, the one practicing would turn around so the other couldn't see.

About 35 years ago, a survey was taken in the U.S. as to who were the best musicians out of all the performers. A cellist came out on top, and I think this is perhaps because a cellist is much more conscious of harmonic changes and implications than a violinist, who is perhaps more concerned with the melodic line and not very interested in what goes on underneath. I think this is a great pity, because they miss a great deal.

In the California Cello Club, we have had just about every great cellist—Casals, Piatigorsky, Rostropovich, [Daniel] Shafran, [Pierre] Fournier. Only one man, Bernie Greenhouse, has ever talked about the bow. They all talked about the left hand, which is something I don't understand, because it's only about 20 percent of your playing. We expect the fingers to be in the right place, of course, but the only other aspect of the left hand worth discussing is intonation. I don't mean by this ordinary intonations; I mean highly specialized intonations that we should play most of the time.

For me, there are 43 notes in an octave. An E♭ flat is not the same as D♯, but we tend to play it in position, so it's always in the same place regardless of the key. I have heard cellists playing D with the first finger in the fourth position on the G string say, "Look, it's exactly in tune with my open D string." But suppose you're in the key E♭. Then it's not going to work. And of course we're plagued with the business of the well tempered.

If you play in the tonality of E minor, your open G and E above it and the open A, then it's going to be miserably out of tune and you'll have to change the E. There are many things like this, and yet the old system seems to stay with us.

There is a difference between good intonation, fine intonation, and magnificent intonation. The most important one, which is never mentioned or thought about, is emotional intonation. There is one place in the Brahms E-Minor Sonata in the first movement, after the second ending, about measure 43. After the big climax, there is a wonderful case of musical exhaustion, with darkness, bruising, hurting. Brahms' notation here indicates the intonation he wants. A little exaggeration on the part of the string player can do wonders, if the player is aware of it. Most players are not. They use that irritating habit of vibrating, regardless of whether or not the intonation will be covered by the vibrato.

I had a discussion with one of my colleagues a while ago, and I said, "At what age do you think you should tell a student about the intricacies of intonation?" We hashed it out, and we thought it probably shouldn't be until students are nearing their 20s. Had I been told when I'd been playing the cello for two or three years that intonation changes according to the key and the emotions, I would have put my cello away and said, "To hell with it," and chosen something else to do.

String players should study singers. We can learn so much more about legato, for example, from the really great singers than from any string player. We hear the various colors and shades in the notes. Think of Chaliapin, who gave six or eight colors in one note. I find that young people will go to hear the great string players of today, and they will almost immediately begin to emulate them, which is not such a good idea. This is one of the reasons Slava [Rostroporich] won't teach with a cello in his hand.

POSITION PLAYING

An aspect of cello playing that intrigues me is why we think in terms of positions. You hear, "You must keep your fingers down and you must play in position." When I was teaching in England 15 years ago, some of the undergraduate students would ask what they could do to get through. "My senior recital was so painful, because they hold our fingers down." Now why do we always have to change positions on the first finger? Why not the second, third, or fourth? Why not the half step? I hear so much badgering about positions, because that's how people have been taught, not because it sounds good. Most cello technique goes against the music in quite an appalling way. One should think entirely of the music and

finger accordingly. I admit it's more trouble—
you probably have to shift twice instead of
once—but it's worth it. One should always shift
on a half step and on the bow change.

Generally fingering is taught in an extremely old-fashioned way. The teaching of positions
should be finished within six months. After
that one shouldn't have to think about it. I hear
people say, "We must play in positions," and it
is so limiting. Often the fingering goes against
the sense of the music, so the sooner one can
forget positions, the better off one is. I have
always wondered why finger exercises start on
the first finger and move up to the fourth and
back again instead of the other way around so
that the fourth finger (being the weakest) can
get the exercise twice instead of the first finger.
Why do we always shift on the first finger and
never on the others?

Colin in 1987;
photograph by
Jennifer Sharpe

At the beginning one has to learn where to put one's fingers down on
the fingerboard, where the notes are, and so we learn the positions. If you
try to teach intonation by position, however, you will achieve only a half-
baked intonation, one that has been not thought through. The fingers are
always going to come down on the same spot on the fingerboard, regardless of the key one is in. I'm speaking mainly about young children, not
professionals, who will automatically make adjustments. A teacher will say,
"That's out of tune" or "That's in tune," but we never elaborate on which
key it's in tune with. If we don't think in positions, the fingers will develop a greater agility, going down on the place that is right for that key, not
"right" according to the fingerboard.

One interesting thing about Heifetz' playing is that he didn't use the
left-hand fingers just by themselves; he threw the fingers by the hand,
which of course gives the playing incredible life. And why should the fingers have to do all the work? To combat the percussive qualities of the
fingers going numb, I think you should always do your descending playing with a slight left-hand pizzicato, which will make it very clear. Also, I
find that playing vibrato right from the fingertip never sounds as good as
if one is playing on the flat of the fingers. It's all right to have rounded fingers for your technical work, but you should flatten out a bit more flesh for
the lyrical, melodic playing. It also helped me to pull the fingers slightly to
the left-hand side. And, on the subject of vibrato, if you play with an
intense, still hand, and then you use the slightest vibrato, it will sound as
if you're using the bow properly. The bow is like a paintbrush; though we
may have excellent paint, we need the right brush stroke.

I have always played octaves between thumb and two rather than thumb and three. I noticed Rostropovich doing the same thing—not that this makes it right or wrong; that's not the point. If you have three fingers down, there is more chance of the third finger moving away from or toward the thumb; whereas if you have just the two, it's easier to keep the feeling of distance. With harmonics also, I would never use the third finger, and I found that putting my finger between the strings gives a sense of security to the finger and to the hand. I don't have to try to keep the weight off, which is especially hard if one is a little nervous.

SPEED AND TIMING

Playing triplets fascinates me, because if one's playing is rhythmically correct, it sounds dead—no movement forward or backward. When I was learning the first quartet of Bloch with Bloch, I had taken great care in the first movement, where there is a short passage in triplets, to see that they were absolutely correct. When we played them through the first time, he yelled, "Don't give me triplets!" Of course, if the composer is using triplets as a matter of tension, that's different.

Spacing is one of the most wonderful aspects of music. A metronome, of course, is absolutely useless, because it cannot tell you the exact psychological moment to put in a note or a beat. A very good example of this is in the theme and variations of the slow movement of Beethoven's Op. 111. The Adagio movement of the last piano sonata is in 3/4, and if it's absolutely even, it's going to sound too slow no matter what speed you play it. If you displace the second beat a little bit so you have more time at the end of the major to give it a sense of movement, you can play any tempo you like, and it will never sound too slow.

I have just finished coaching the fourth Beethoven Sonata, and I'm always puzzled by people's lack of observation of Beethoven's marks. I'm thinking in particular of a place in the first andante before the allegro, where there is a crescendo from the end of the sixth into the fifth. It goes only to the first 16th note and not the A, as everybody plays it.

I don't know how much of this is coming out of America. When Zubin Mehta had his 50th birthday, there was a special concert in New York in his honor. Isaac Stern and Itzhak Perlman played a double concerto, and it was a tragedy. All the tempi were New York and had nothing to do with the period in which the piece was written, and both violins were trying to outplay each other. Much that comes out of New York is just so much playacting, which is a way of catching an audience, but an artist should not descend to this level. Let the music be pure.

SCALES, TRILLS, AND
OTHER FUNDAMENTALS

I want to mention the beauty of scales. This, to me, is fascinating: It is important that children be taught their scales. Scales are what all music is about. I think scales can be beautiful as fine pieces of music. What can be more beautiful than a major scale played with wonderful intonation? Perhaps more beautiful are the melodic and harmonic scales, but they need a very, very fine intonation. If you practice them this way, then you are onto something, the discovery that scales have their own extraordinary beauty. But if we think scales are an exercise, then they become a horrible burden, and no wonder kids hate to practice them! But I think children often are not shown the intricacies, all the beauties, and that for me is very important.

We don't pay enough attention to the indications the composer writes. We read allegro, andante, andante con moto, and so on, but if there is anything else after that, we don't really take it in. Oh, it's fast! Oh, it's slow! Let's play! Think of the two composers who indicated most clearly what they wanted: Beethoven and Bloch. Beethoven's indications in the 32 piano sonatas are a model of understanding his own emotions and his own knowledge of how he wants something played. Most string players, unfortunately, don't find this out because they don't play the piano. They are not interested in anything other than their own instrument, and they don't go to hear other recitals; a cellist won't go to a violin recital unless it's a soloist with a huge name. This is wrong. In one of the piano sonatas there is a slow movement marked Adagio, sempre sostenuto. We ignore the sempre sostenuto, which is the whole point of the movement. That is a very big mistake.

Trills can be a great bugbear, especially on the C string of the cello, where you have a hefty string to press down. For many years I suffered an inability to play trills, largely due to the German school of cello playing as it was taught to me. "When you play trills you have to play with a very strong trilling finger," which is nonsense. All it does is to make you slower and slower. Being young, I was afraid to try anything on my own, though perhaps I was more of a rebel than some. I remember asking two people about trilling. One was Myra Hess, who had one of the most liquid, limpid trills imaginable and a very physically strange way of playing them, because the wrist would be below the keyboard. She had a wonderful trill, and I asked her one day in a rehearsal, "Myra, how do you trill this way?" She said, "Think of two notes: don't play fast, but play evenly." The other one was Casals. I asked him one day how he did his trills. He simply said, "You hold the note down, and with the trilling finger above it, you play a little bit sharp, a little bit high, and then you don't bother to put the string

all the way down. Just flutter your finger, but keep your bow strong."
Within ten minutes I had a trill. I mention this because I've met so many
youngsters who had the same problem.

Apart from teaching a few bow strokes, most teachers don't understand
the nuances of bowing. So little thought is usually given to which part of
the bow you're in, the sort of technique you want to use, the varying of
speeds, knowing when you want to vary them, and so on. For example,
the speed of the bow is rarely the same all the way through the stroke. If
there is a run, the player thinks about the left hand and does not use the
bow and therefore loses the clarity he could get so easily. Bowing should
be according to what the music demands—the right type of bowing, the
right speeds of bow for the emotion of the music, the right intonation that
suits that moment in the music.

Along the same lines, people don't think about vibrato. It's just something they learn when they're kids, and it's like a disease that you can't get
rid of once you get it. People don't think in terms of different speeds and
different sizes, which is absolutely imperative. The mixture of the bow and
the vibrato and the position on the string—if all these things are right, you
can do so much; and if they're wrong, your playing will never be anything
but half-baked. I don't think it is possible to discuss real cello playing
unless one realizes these fundamentals.

QUARTET PLAYING

As a cellist, I was always taught that the cello was the foundation of a quartet. In certain aspects it is, I think, but not in playing. If the cello is the
foundation, the others will get dragged down by cello-featured concrete.
The heavy bass will feel immovable, without life. I prefer to think of the
cello as being the springboard. You play a note with energy, taking away a
little bit afterward, so that you give an upward spring to the people playing above you. This is important. I hear so many quartets in which the
sound is retained. It should move a little, so that it does not become heavy
and, as Tovey would say, "glutinous."

Another important aspect of quartet playing is the projection of sound,
which seems to me to be something that is not given enough importance
in teaching. In a Brahms scherzo, for example, one of the inner parts,
perhaps the viola or the second fiddle, has a melody that is covered by the
top part or two parts. The lower part can get lost if the player is not good
at the art of projecting sound. A little edge will help to cut through. I do
think that it's worth losing something for the overall line, because the line
is the most important part of all. Take, for example, the last movement of
the "American" Quartet of Dvořák when it's building up to a huge surge of

The Grillers circa 1947

excitement. I often hear the violin becoming more exciting and the whole quartet building, but they will go so far and then realize they can't give any more, so they cut back to *mf* and then go off again. This is so theatrical. It spoils the line, the whole design, the structure. It is always possible to dig out a little more, and if it's created well, no artifice is needed. This is another of the many little beefs I have with quartet playing.

Of course, there are millions of small things. Players sometimes have problems with composers. I think of the Adagio and Fugue of Mozart, the one taken from the two piano sonatas, where the fugue is so busy all the way through. In every part there is something of importance, almost costantly, and each player thinks, "I must bring this out; it's impotant." Everybody has something, and the result is that it gets thicker and thicker and less clear. The more one tries to bring something out, the less out it comes! It's always wiser, with very busy works, just to cut it down to something quite small in sound, because the musical argument will come through much better.

In string quartet playing, one must realize that intonation is moveable. It has to move by key. It is a big help to have the viola and cello tune their G strings high, and even a little on the C strings. This brings the

A formal portrait of
the Griller Quartet

top and bottom closer. In the key of F major, for example, which is about the hardest key for a string quartet, one open A string on the violin is enough to set the whole bass high, and it has to be. In Dvořák's "American" Quartet, for example, the viola has many open C's, which will sound miserably flat if the player doesn't put his finger on it to sharpen it. You have to be ready to change your intonation no matter how you were taught.

Sometimes I hear quartets that have been together for a few weeks or a few months, and they have a certain amount of intonation and tone quality by this time. But it is not a quartet, and I don't think it can be for a long time, perhaps for several years. It is not easy to become a real quartet. You have to know each other and know how each one will react under certain circumstances. It takes a long time to match colors—I won't say vibratos necessarily, because they can be different. If somebody has a melody and the others play with the same vibrato, the effect can be nauseating. The others should back off a little bit, be less important. And how few people seem to realize that the dynamic marks should be applied to both hands! It makes a vast difference. One has to find color, shades of sound, different aspects of playing all the time, and all of this takes many years. No matter how well a quartet gets off the ground at the beginning, it's not going to amount to too much for a while.

I've had more than one student say, "Well, of course, what I really want to do is to play in a quartet." I don't say much. We talk around it a bit, and usually in the end they say, "Well, what I would like to do is to get a good college job that pays well and then start a quartet." This is exactly the wrong way around, as far as I'm concerned. To be hired by a university and to be a professional quartet attached to a school, surely you have to be good. You can't expect, "Here's the money, you're worth it," before you have founded a quartet. But this is a money-making prospect these days, which astounds me. I was brought up in the hard school, in the days when no school had a quartet, so you had to make it! The only means you had of earning a living was doing a concert. That was doing it the hard way, and I wouldn't wish it on anybody today, but I do think the attitude, "I'll get a job at a school, and then I'll start a quartet" is backward.

UPKEEP OF THE CELLO

The bridge should be checked about once a month to make sure it is in the proper position, which is slanting back a little bit, not forward. An occasional adjustment will save many a warped bridge. Get your luthier to check your soundpost once in a while. Never do it yourself. I made a vow years ago never to touch a soundpost and have never broken that vow. If you think you can do it, you may be a little rough, and you may split the top or the back and wreck the value of the cello. People in America have a bug about the bass bar. They think it should be replaced about every five years. Sheer rot! This is just a money-making device. The Amati cello I had all my life had the same bass bar for 75 years. Regrettably, during the war, the neck at the shoulder broke off in the bitter cold weather. Hills patched it up for me. They couldn't put a new one in, because it was wartime and they did not have the craftsmen. It lasted a few years this way, but finally, over here in San Francisco, it pulled out, and I had to have a new neck put in. The butchers I took it to, who supposedly were the best people here, put in a new neck, did a very nice job, and without asking me, put in a new bass bar. Was I mad! They put it in straight, which it shouldn't have been, and for the next three months I had to borrow a cello because I couldn't play on the Amati. I finally went back to England and Hills put another one in for me. "Leave well alone!" was the advice they gave me, and it was the best advice I've had.

This reminds me of a violinist who was about to give a recital in London. Two or three weeks beforehand, she began to get very apprehensive and began to think, "Oh my goodness, my fiddle is not sounding." She rushed down to Hills and commanded, "Do something! It's not sounding at all! It doesn't play!" Hills said, "All right, just leave it with us for a couple of days, then come back, and it will be ready for you." The artist went back in a few days and was given the fiddle. She checked it and said, "Ah, wonderful! You are masters, you have done wonders with it!" All they had done, however, was take the violin out shortly before her return, and clean and polish it.

Years ago I had a call from Zara Nelsova, who said she was having great trouble with her cello and that it wasn't sounding in the upper register. I said, "Zara, it's all in the upper register." There was a silence, and she said, "What do you mean?" And I said, "It's all in the upper register. Leave it alone, Zara!" She didn't like that! But that's all right. Sometimes it's all in the imagination.

Regarding the pegs for tuning: I'm against the fine tuners, as they call them, but the pegs should be fitted beautifully. One should be able to tune just as easily and comfortably with the peg as with a fine tuner. The

Colin with Margaret
Rowell, cofounder
(with Colin) of the
California Cello Club,
1986; photograph by
Judy Lepire

reason I think it is better, for a cellist anyway, is that very few of us can reach down there while bowing. It's very hard to keep an evenly flowing bow balanced equally on both strings to get absolute perfection of tuning. If your pegs are well fitted, there should be no problem. When I was a student and had gone in for a lesson with ill-fitting pegs, I would be told to get out and not come back until they were fitted properly. Get it done if you can.

We also don't think very often about the fingerboard. We do worry about the fifths, whether they're good or bad. It's hard to get perfect fifths. Also, people often pair two metal with two gut strings. I've never had any luck getting good fifths between the D and G strings if one is metal and the other is gut. If your fingerboard is pitted, which will happen with much playing, you will never get good fifths. The fingerboard gets a little dent in it, and you can't press the string all the way down, so you get uneven pressure. If your fifths are not quite perfect, don't go through the tortures of the damned with the left-hand fingers going backward and forward. You can do it by lifting, so that the pressure can vary on one string or the other—a much better way of doing it.

Keep your cello clean. Dust it down once a week. Cellos tend to get black over the years with the rosin caked on them. Wipe off the rosin every few weeks with a little rubbing alcohol. Scotch, vodka, gin, or any spirit will do it, but it's a waste of good stuff!

OLD AND NEW

Two or three years ago I was in England, and Bonnie had asked me to get the Triple Concerto of Tippett, so I tracked it down and bought it. The manager came out when she heard someone was buying it, and she asked all kinds of questions: Who was it for? Where were they, and why did they want it? I said a cellist in California wanted to play it. She was very interested and offered me a recording of it. I asked, "How much will that be?" and she said, "I'll give it to you." She gave me a tape, and I was very interested to hear it when I got back to California. Playing the tape and looking at the score, I was struck deeply by the fact that old-fashioned playing won't work in modern pieces. Somebody new is needed. The old way of getting from position to position doesn't sound right, the tone quality doesn't sound right, and the vibrato doesn't sound right. I don't want to think very much about it; this is for a younger person to do. But this matter has brought string playing into focus for me.

Cello playing has had a tremendous ascendancy over violin playing the last few years. Perhaps 30 or 40 years ago the violin was king, and the cello was an also-ran. Many of the technical devices we used we took from violin playing out of admiration and envy. I don't think a lot of them work, but I don't think a lot of the modern playing works: it's old-fashioned technique against modern music. I'm not sure that the Galamian influence has been a very good one. It's been very strong in the East in this country and has spread; I think most of the first chairs of string sections are Galamian students. They consistently use a hard-hitting spiccato, which is all right in its place, perhaps in Bartók, but I don't think it is right in Mozart and Haydn. Perhaps Galamian was the culmination or zenith of the old Russian school, as Bach was the culmination of a period. This has left a tremendous mark of hysteria in playing, which is an impossible situation. It is like playacting, which is so common these days. And what is this urgency, this nuclear fiddle playing? Have we lost our acceptance of life, which must have its dull periods as well as its exciting ones? We've lost the serenity and the beauty, the wide scope of emotions in music. We seem to have come to a point where we have to take drugs to make it exciting, and sooner or later we reach insensibility and death. Music shouldn't be this way. The emotions in Bach are not the agonies of a moment. In Bach, Beethoven, Brahms, there is a distillation of emotions, so their music achieves the right perspective. These agonies are not an unbearable hurt. They bring philosophy and acceptance, not panic.

This is like the situation in education. There is an enormous stress put on education in America. To my way of thinking, it is the wrong stress and the wrong sort of education. Much of it should be and will be changed eventually. Here people get education to get a well-paid job instead of for pleasure or further understanding or the fruition of an idea. People buy education like we buy meals. If we pay a lot, then it's good, even though we can't tell the difference between that and the shop next door slinging hash. Just because it is expensive and you get a piece of paper, Americans seem to think that education is the answer to everything, but I do not believe it is. It is used incorrectly.

It is the same with performers. I remember Bloch talking about a performance of *Meistersinger* he heard once in Germany in which there were no great singers, no great orchestra, and no great conductor. But he said it was the finest Wagner he had ever heard because it had the whole essence of *Meistersinger*. Today we think we can hear it only with world-renowned singers performing for astronomical fees; otherwise we are not interested. This is wrong, and it also means that the young person doesn't get a chance.

Colin circa 1947

Teaching and Learning

5

AT THE UNIVERSITY LEVEL, WHAT IS TAUGHT in music departments is not so much the instruments as a general attitude toward music. Unfortunately, people get an idea and stay with it no matter what. They try to make the music fit the idea rather than the other way around. Teachers all have their own opinions, and they want to keep and protect their little ideas. Let me quote [teacher] George Santayana reflecting on faculty meetings (in Byden, Flemming, Handlin, and Fernstrom's *Glimpses of the Harvard Post,* published by Harvard University near the turn of the century). He says, "The faculty meetings were an object lesson to me in the futility of parliamentary institutions. Those who spoke, spoke badly with imperfect knowledge of the matter in hand and simply to air their prejudices. The rest hardly listened. If there was a vote, it revealed not the results of the debate but the previous and settled sentiments of the voters. The uselessness and the poor quality of the whole performance was so evident that it surprised me to see that so many intelligent men, for they were intelligent men doing very special work, should tamely waste so much time in keeping up the farce."

This sums up the situation in schools. It doesn't take into consideration that most schools do not like having big names on their faculties; they prefer mediocrity, because they feel safer that way. Here at Berkeley we had Bukofzer, who was eminent in the field of musicology, as well as ourselves (the Griller Quartet) as performers. They disliked having us very much. When Ernest Bloch was on the faculty, two or three other faculty members got together and wrote a letter to the president complaining about him. Sproul, being a wise man, wrote back and said, "What's wrong with my music faculty that they can't get on with Ernest Bloch?" I think, as Casals said about Tovey, Bloch was the loneliest man in the world of music, because everybody was afraid of him.

In America everybody expects to go to college, which I think puts education in the wrong perspective. Most people go because it's a means to earning a living. To me a university is for serious scholarly study, not for learning how to run a hotel. The result is that the universities are crammed full of nonentities, people who are probably not going to make anything, people who don't know what to do. It becomes a way of life, like joining a church or the air force.

Some people think a good method of teaching is to shock people. One person on the faculty here started a series of lectures on Schubert songs. At the very first lecture, he turned to the class and said, "Schubert never wrote a decent song in his life." Now, this is provocative and stupid. There should be some love and admiration for these wonderful songs that should come through to the people, not just putting yourself up to be clever. One day this teacher said to Jack, my second fiddle, "Of course you know, Jack, that music has three functions: first to be written, second to be analyzed, and last to be heard." Jack replied, "Oh dear, I suppose that's why when Mozart wrote his six quartets dedicated to Haydn, he picked up his manuscript and a fiddle and they went down to Haydn's house to play them."

I had a student who was in her third or fourth year at Mills to whom I was trying to explain something about Bach one day. I could hear the wheels start to go around in her head. "Oh yes, that must have been last year in the second semester, and I think it was the third chapter in the book we were reading, and it says this, that, and the other." Then she couldn't play anything because it had become too cerebral; instinct had been excluded. This is a danger of education: it can educate the essence out of you. I am very much in favor of study, but one has to be careful not to believe everything one is told. Each of us is beckoned toward the arts, and in each one of us is what I call a little bit of the Godhead, a Something that appeals to us, reaches to a part of us that we don't normally know about. You could call it instinct, but it is more than instinct, that spark, and if you let it be educated out of you, you have lost the most valuable thing in the world. Keep it, nurse it, nurture it, never lose it.

We tend to adore our teachers and think they're gods, and we tend to take the lazy way out and do what we're told without thinking. We need confirmation in a book on the subject, and yet musicologists tend to miss the inner meaning. Tovey was an exception. But we still have to think, to find out for ourselves how something is done. Experiment in your practice for all you're worth. Don't believe everything you're told. Hang on to the Godhead. I feel very strongly on this subject because I've seen so much nonsense.

Many junior and senior high schools here have school orchestras, and the school music teacher has an impossible job. He has to do it all: teach strings, violin, viola, cello, bass, all the wind instruments, the choir. This is outrageous. I have myself have had to teach string players who have six weeks on the fiddle, six weeks on the viola, and six weeks on the cello.

Then they're ready to go out and teach! What can they know? It's ridiculous. It's better not to learn at all than to learn under those conditions. I'm against schools in music. I'm against the arts in universities. I do not think they belong there, any more than I think business schools or learning how to cook belong in universities. Vocational schools are for that sort of thing. Many of the people who go to university should instead be in vocational school.

SUZUKI

I've just completed a week of master classes, or workshops. I hate the term master classes. Many thoughts came to my mind about the short-comings of teaching, especially the teaching of children, and in particular the Suzuki method. I admit that I have not really studied the method, and my acquaintance with it is through other teachers and talking to children. However, it seems to me the Suzuki method fails badly by not teaching the children their notes. I cannot conceive why they don't do this. Isn't it just as easy for children as learning their ABCs? It becomes very hard when they learn them too late. I have heard 16-year-olds say, "Damn Suzuki; I'll never be able to sight-read." I think the method has enabled teachers to take up teaching when they shouldn't be teaching. When you teach, you have to apply a large amount of psychology. Every person is an individual, and you therefore cannot teach with a method. It won't hold up.

It is also a mistake to start children so young; surely they are worthy of having childhood. This is such a wonderful part of their lives, the only time they are not beset by worries. I met a woman the other day in a luthier's shop who was looking for a violin for her three-year-old daugter. Three years is much too young. It would be better to start children at seven. They'll get on just as fast and have those wonderful years to daydream, which no kid these days is allowed time to do. They need a little peace and quiet and some childhood. Furthermore, this sort of thing smacks horribly of letting the parents have their way. So many parents suffer from thwarted ambitions, and they seek fulfillment through their children. They become hideously ambitious, especially the mothers. They start children earlier and earlier and tax the child beyond endurance. The mom becomes the kingpin. She runs her family, runs the children, and gets the idea that nothing could go on without her. She is indispensable. The children get enough authority—"Clean your teeth, make your bed, change your clothes"—and then to practice with your mother practicing alongside! I call it smotherhood.

Portrait of Colin
Hampton, 1990;
photograph by
Judy Lepire

In addition, the Suzuki method is imitative, and this is not appropriate, at least for the Western person. A child should have something outside of the home, away from the family, something in which the parents do not take any part. This way the child feels his individuality, feels he's on his own, with a teacher, a person outside the family. Tremendous love, affection, faith, and trust can grow between the teacher and the student. Children may not confide their innermost feelings to a mother for fear of ridicule or betrayal. Having the mother present at lessons blocks any close relationship between teacher and pupil. I have experienced this many times. One pupil I had was an 11-year-old girl whose mother defied me when I asked her not to attend the lesson. She came four or five times, and the daughter got tighter and tighter, until finally I asked the mother to leave us alone. The mom was hardly out of earshot when the little girl turned and said, "Thank you so much. My mother is such a bitch!" Of course, she would never have said that with her mother there.

Anne Crowden has a very good violinist who is 15 years old. The child's day is arranged for her from the moment she gets up in the morning until she goes to bed at night. She has no time for herself, no time to daydream, which to me is one of the most important things in the world. This is apparent in Beethoven and many other composers. It's essential. This particular child at the age of 15 looks like a little old lady. It's pathetic.

Teaching has so much to do with the attitude of the parents. Incidentally, many of the great artists have not been very happy individuals. Heifetz, for example, on his eighth birthday received a bicycle from his father. When his father came home from work and asked, "Have you done your six hours of practice today, Jascha?" he got the reply, "No, I've only done four. I was out on the bike." He never saw that bike again.

On the other hand, I had a very nice relationship with a student named Izumi, a little Japanese girl, who was ten when she came to me for help with piano and composition. We had a wonderful friendship. Izumi would open up any discussion, and she would talk about what she felt like. This most likely would not have happened if her mother had been there during the lessons.

LEARNING PIANO

I deplore the fact that most string students do not play the piano. Speaking as a teacher, I think the piano should be compulsory. I have found that those who have piano are much easier to teach than those who don't. They learn faster, and they are much quicker with intervals, partly because they can see them, of course. I deplore the fact that in general so many people learning instruments show an interest only in the instrument they are learning. Violinists will learn their literature, to a certain extent; cellists will do likewise; pianists likewise. But what about all the great music for other instruments that we do not know, thereby depriving ourselves of being very fine all-round musicians? This is what we need. Otherwise we cannot know as much about music as we should. How many violinists or cellists will go to hear the Beethoven piano sonatas, or bother to learn them, especially if they haven't learned piano? If they have a certain amount of piano, no matter how plodding they are, they can get to know them, by all means, this way (not for concert performance, of course).

I have long admired the conductor who can sit down at a piano with a full score of a new symphony that he doesn't know and be able to reduce it mentally, so that he can not only read the clefs and key signatures but can make sense out of it. Even pianists cannot read scores structurally, harmonically, or contrapuntally. They don't know what to leave out or what to put in. This seems to me to be a severe loss, especially when they are sight-reading a piece. Their sight-reading is, as a rule, not very good, simply because they don't have the opportunity that people playing orchestral instruments have to do a lot of sight-reading. Pianists don't get these opportunities, but they could make up for it by doing a certain amount of sight-reading daily. I've seen so many of them come to a difficult moment and immediately leave out the left hand and fill in the florid writing, which is just the bit we can do without. We need the harmonic fill-in, which is usually in the left hand. They also don't know how to read voice chords on sight, because they don't know harmonically what they are. They can't see it. This is, I suppose, a lack of training, but I think it is very important.

I once had a bass player come in with a cello sonata of Vivaldi and give the piano part to the pianist, who read it as it was in the score. This, of course, wouldn't do at all, because the whole thing changed. When I asked why he didn't leave out certain things or put them in a different octave, I was faced with absolute inability to do this. This happens, I think, because they cannot see harmonically what the chords are, what the progressions are. If pianists also played a string instrument, they would have a much greater understanding of playing chamber music, not only for playing legato, but for matching sounds and knowing exactly the amount of support to give underneath. Of the hundreds of pianists we played with in our lives, the one that stood out miles above the rest was Myra Hess, who did have an innate understanding of these things. One of the reasons [Vladimir] Horowitz is great is that he does not play with one hand accompanying the other, as so many pianists do, thereby missing so many wonderful things. He reads music like a score, four or five parts, whatever it might be.

Another aspect of piano playing that is often so poor—no doubt due to the fact that pianists are reared very strongly on Romantic music, Chopin, Schumann, and Brahms—is that the pedal goes down and is left down. This is possibly right for Romantic music but wrong for the classics, and yet they still do the same thing. It seems to me when Beethoven writes rests, where Mozart and Haydn write rests, they mean it! It is an awful nuisance to write rests! One of the great examples of this is Op. 110 of Beethoven. Just before going into the last inverted fugue, he puts the pedal down, and he marks staccato chords with triplet rests. It must have been an enormous struggle for him to write all that, and yet people come along and play, not observing the rests. And it can be done, still pedaling and making the semblance of rests. But people won't do it. I talk to piano teachers about that, and their argument is, "Oh, the piano doesn't sound." Well, likely not the way they would expect it to sound, but maybe it was the way a fortepiano was expected to sound. I rather agree with Tovey, who said it was the greatest impudence to change Beethoven.

EDITIONS

Editions are one of my big bugbears. I am appalled at some of the editions that exist. Take Leonard Rose, for example. I hate to speak against him, since he was a good friend and a nice man and a good cellist, but his editions are appalling. He has no concern for the composer; he thinks entirely from the cello point of view. He even changes Brahms' phrasings to get in a slide. It staggers me that anybody could be so oblivious of what the composer desires. After all, Brahms was no fool; he knew the instrument and he had [Robert] Hausmann to help him. Hausmann must have been a fine cellist, and a fine musician. It's thanks to Hausmann that Brahms revised the E-Minor Sonata, and it's thanks entirely to Hausmann for the F-Major Sonata. Who is Rose to come along and change things?

One of the important points about editions, from the player's point of view, is never to take things from the cello or violin part but always from the piano score. You will find that all the ideas the editor puts in the cello part, he doesn't bother to put in the piano part, thank God, and we can get somewhere near what the composer wanted this way. We have far too many German editions left over from the days of [Julius] Klengel, [F.W.] Grutzmacher, [Hugo] Becker, and other awful people. They finger absolutely in position, which is anathema to me because it stops all the imaginative fingering that one can do and always goes against the music. They love to finger in patterns. But then when they get into difficulties, there are no fingerings! So when we need their help, it is not there. I think it will be many years before we get over the terrible German editing and the German way of playing the cello.

Something that had intrigued me on the basis of Casals' recommending it was the Hausman edition of the Bach Suites, which Casals said was the best edition you could get. I hunted for it for about 30 years and never could find it. Then Enrique Jorda was our conductor here at the San Francisco Symphony for about seven years, and before he left, his wife, Audrey,

Colin with sons Andrew (left) and Ian (right)

called me up and said, "Colin, my father was a cellist and I've always taken his music wherever I've gone, but I guess I can't take it with me anymore. Would you like it?" I went over and spent the whole day with Audrey, sitting on the floor and going through all her father's cello music. It was not out of the ordinary—the everyday Golterman concertos, études, and so on. And then we came across the first edition of the Brahms E-Minor Sonata and finally the Bach Hausmann edition.

I do believe it's a very fine one. The structure is very important in the Bach Suites—where the structural points are, where the modulations are, which keys you're going through, and so on, because intonation must vary by key, and if you know the structural and harmonic points, and where pedal points start and finish, then you know a little about how to play it. If you are playing over a pedal point, you can't hang around; it's a driving force. Any curtailing of phrases should be done more by dynamics than by rallentandos, not holding out notes that are really unimportant. It's hard to get across to a student that one has to think of these suites harmonically. I've always been struck by the fact that cellists nearly always play the tune because they don't know how to harmonize. This seems to me a sad lack of taking responsibility for the instrument as well as poor knowledge as a musician. Only the other night I was doing a workshop, and one of the cellists played the "Courante" from the Sixth Suite. I asked, "Do you know what this is?" and he replied, "It's a dance." I said, "Well, that's a little bit vague. Can you fill me in a bit?" And he didn't have the slightest idea what sort of a dance it was; therefore, of course, he didn't really know what sort of interpretation to make. If you are performing Bach Suites you must know these kinds of things.

GREAT COMPOSERS

It seems to me that the Haydn quartets don't reach that height of won-drous beauty that Mozart does, but they're much more interesting. Haydn had an incredible imagination. Mozart's string quartets are wonderful music, but most of the writing is not very interesting. The *Seven Last Words* of Haydn to me is one of the great works, imaginatively handled, consid-ering he did it with a string quartet—just four voices in a very simple way, but with incredible inspiration and religious fervour. I would put it on a par with the *St. Matthew Passion* any day.

Beethoven, of course, had a vivid imagination and incredible emotions, constantly changing. My favorites are Opp. 127 and 132. Most people, I think, would go for the C♯Minor, but 127 seems to me the epitome of what love should be. From start to finish it gets more and more wonderful. And 132 is incredibly passionate. To me Beethoven also has a wonderful sense of austerity. When I use this word I'm often misunderstood. I mean aus-terity in the sense of pure and basic emotion, breathtaking. I don't know of any other composer who can do quite the same thing.

Three times over the years I asked Ernest Bloch who he considered to be the three greatest composers. Each time he told me Bach, Beethoven, and Wagner—not always in that order. He used to get very upset with the anti-Wagner people. He called them shrimps, and he considered them unworthy to lick Wagner's boots.

Over the years I asked a variety of people—musicians or not—who they considered to be the eight or ten most important composers, and I noticed the same omission every time, which was Handel. Only one per-son ever mentioned him, which is rather strange when you consider Beethoven thought he was so important. And he was important, but some-how his music doesn't stay in our memories.

It's interesting how music goes in and out of fashion. Bach wasn't played for 150 years after his death, so Mozart knew only the *Christmas Oratorio* and a few of the 48. Consider that in Bach's day it was imperative to attend church. It was very serious. You didn't go for a quick service but for a ser-mon of an hour to an hour and a half. Can you imagine the wheelwright and the candlestick maker having to face a Bach Cantata, another hour and a half of music? They must have hated Bach! I can see why he was-n't played for such a long time.

So Bach went out of fashion. Palestrina was out for quite a while. Bloch is out right now. Mendelssohn went out for a while. Then there was the extraordinary situation of Brahms. For about 40 years Brahms was con-sidered a rather minor composer; the best pieces he wrote were the songs. This is nuts! Time will tell whether a work is great or not. We always have to allow for that hiatus to see if something will come back.

SOUL AND SPIRIT

As I grow older, I find myself questioning so much, and I find myself much more into the mysticism of the music. The first time we flew to Australia and back, we were going over Persia and Bahrain, and the weather was very clear. We could look down and see the sorts of houses people had built. Everything was in squares and cubes, and I came to the conclusion that men think this way; they build towns in this way, especially in America. I think mentally, and possibly physically, they feel safer; also, we all tend to do what others do. I have noticed this in performances of the normal repertoire. Everyone copies each other, doing fancy things that really have nothing to do with the music, and then they miss the really important aspects. They break the line with some cute thing that is perfectly horrible to me.

Recently I got a book called *The Seventh Dragon: The Riddle of Equal Temperament* [Anita Sullivan; Lake Oswego, Oregon: Metamorphous Press, 1985], which discusses the well-tempered clavier. I hadn't realized that ornamentation started because of what is called the mean tuning on a keyboard where they could play only two, three, or four keys. Ornamentation covered the bad intonation. Perhaps we are using ideas and techniques whose purpose is no longer necessary. English music, for example, Purcell or Vaughan Williams, will not stand up well to putting in glissandi. The emotion is already clearly written into the music, and it will not take this sort of frosting. Kreisler, of course, was the past master, but it seems to me that Heifetz also does this.

Now, having reached the ripe old age of 75, I am not so interested in cello playing, and I am not interested in Talents. Yes, they can make me pleased and happy, but I can't get excited about them. Cello playing, as such, does not hold much interest for me. I *am* interested in, and I do find myself being more and more attracted to, the spiritual side—not *my* spiritual side, but the spiritual side of Brahms, Beethoven, Bach, and others. This spiritual part is the hard part to find, to understand. Maybe one should not try to understand it. Perhaps I am spoiling the whole thing and I shouldn't bother, but a wonderful spiritual experience, or emotional feeling, can be inspired by music. You can write a book about it, and get a job at a university, and spoil everything! These things can only be felt and dimly understood.

In Brahms, I find that the most spiritual movements are always the inner two. Mozart, of course, wrote God-sent melodies, almost childlike in their simplicity and beauty—like the Italian painter Santa Croce, a Catholic who painted so simply, with very simple colors but with tremendous fervor. Mozart is a little bit like this, though the emotions are so deep and so childlike. Bach, I think, is more in control of his emotions, beyond

Colin working on
his *Holy Sonnets*,
June 1996

other composers. You feel his defenses are very strong, and they store up, hold in, and *support* the very deep emotions that he has. With Beethoven and Brahms, their agony is greater because their support is not so great; therefore the agony comes through more to the listener. Perhaps I am more receptive to this sort of music. I think of Op. 127 of Beethoven, the passion and the agony in the first and last movements, and of course the celestial beauty of the slow movement.

It is interesting that with Brahms' chamber music, the larger the group, the more double-stops he uses. Fascinating! Why are the Sixth Bach Suite and Beethoven's A-Major Sonata considered the greats? Beethoven's last two sonatas are greater, but the A-Major is the one that everybody wants to play. Bach's Sixth Suite is hard to bring off. I don't think I've ever heard a fine performance of it. I must admit I have not heard Lazlo Varga play it on his five-string cello, but I think this is the only way to bring it off! When people speak with bated breath about this suite, is it because it is great music or because it is so difficult to play on four strings? The only way you can resolve the argument is to play it on the piano, not on the cello, where the technical difficulties do not intrude on one's judgment. The Suite is not as great as No. 5 or No. 2, but it is endlessly passionate, a dark and brooding work.

I ask these questions and never know the answers. Nobody will. It will be a dreadful day when we do know all the answers. It bothers me that the scientists are always searching for the cause of everything. When man has discovered everything there is, he will have no more reason to live. It is the mystery of things that keeps us going. Once we understand it, that will be the end of it.

Tenor voice

213 DEIGN AT MY HANDS THIS CROWN OF PRAYER AND PRAISE

violin solo

con sord *pp*

Cello

Bass

217

221

225

AFTERWORD

At the close of the Griller Quartet's career, Colin made a courageous decision: he would not play professionally anymore. "For 35 years, we were kings for a night in whatever community we were playing before moving on. It is now time to settle down and become part of a community and participate in it."

At 50, Colin decided to develop other aspects of his musicianship. He was a chamber music coach par excellence; his musical and psychological insight made him a great teacher. Though there was a constant stream of visitors to his house, Colin reserved a daily portion of his time to what he referred to as his "work." He was not so much alluding to his many arrangements for cello ensemble but to the process of composition, which was deeply satisfying to him.

Colin composed all his life. During his performing years, he kept it very quiet, but later, in the privacy of his home, he began to share his creative ideas and write specifically for his friends and students. He was not ambitious about his compositions; he once laughingly remarked, "There's enough bad music in the world already." For Colin, composition was a spiritual quest. He was a passionate man who felt strongly about what he valued. Though not an admirer of organized religion, Colin was acutely aware of the spiritual threads that run through our lives. "There is a little of the Godhead in each of us," he said. "It is up to us to reveal its potency."

Colin's *Holy Sonnets of John Donne for Tenor and Strings* was premiered at a concert by the Crowden School of music in Berkeley, California, celebrating Colin's 85th birthday in 1996. Colin was thrilled with the concert and wrote to Anne Crowden, "You have given me my first chance to be what I have always wanted to be. . . . My heartfelt thanks to you, Anne, for granting me my lifelong ambition in such a wonderful way." The concert was a timely acknowledgment of Colin's creative life. He died just two months later, leaving a rich legacy and an appreciative community of students, colleagues, family, and friends.

Ian Hampton

COLIN HAMPTON
CHRONOLOGY

1911 Born, Brompton Road, London
1923 Herbert Walenn Cello School;
      attended Westminster Choir School
1927 Royal Academy of Music;
      future quartet coached by Lionel Tertis
1928 Griller Quartet debut, London
1930 First tour of Europe
1934 Married Elspeth Swanson
1938–39 New York debut; first U.S. tour
1940 Quartet in the RAF; contract with Decca
1947 Visit to Music Academy of the West
1949 Resident at University of California, Berkeley
1950 Founded California Cello Club
1953 Married Bonnie Bell
1953 25th-anniversary concert,
      Royal Festival Hall, London
1957 Broke contract with Decca;
      began recording with Vanguard
1960 Casals master classes, Berkeley
1961 Quartet disbanded after
      the death of Philip Burton
1962 Casals masterclasses, Berkeley
1968 Married Megan Dalton
1996 Died after short illness

GRILLER QUARTET DISCOGRAPHY

Beethoven: Op. 95; Op. 132 (Decca).

Beethoven: Op. 95; Op. 18, No. 3 (Decca).

Bliss: Quartet No. 3. Sibelius. *Voces Intimae* (Decca).

Bliss: Quartet in B Flat (Decca).

Bliss: Quintet for Clarinet and Strings. With
    Frederick Thurston (Clarinet Classics #5, UK).

Bloch: Quartets 1–5 (Decca).

Dvořák: Op. 96 (Decca).

Ferguson: Octet (Decca).

Haydn: Op. 3, No. 5; Op. 51, *Seven Last Words of Christ;*
    Op. 103; Op. 33, No. 3 (Decca).

Haydn: String Quartets, Opp. 71 and 74
    (Vanguard Classics 2- Van 62).

Mozart: Adagio and Fugue; the "Hunt" Quartet;
    Horn Quintet; G-Minor Viola Quintet.
    With Dennis Brain, French horn;
    Max Gilbert, viola (Decca).

Mozart: Quintet for Horn, Violin, 2 Violas,
    and Cello in E Flat Major, K. 407.
    With Dennis Brain, horn (Pearl, Koch 26).

Mozart: Adagio and Fugue; String Quintets
    K. 516, K. 593. With William Primrose, viola
    (Vanguard Classics OVC 8024 ADD).

Mozart: String Quintets K. 406, K. 515, K. 614.
    With William Primrose, viola
    (Vanguard Classics OVC 8025).

COLIN HAMPTON'S COMPOSITIONS

Published Works for Cello Ensemble
Hymn to Saint Cecilia for Massed Celli
The Ring of Brodgar for Six Celli
Requiem for Six Celli
Pedal Points and Textures for Seven Celli
Comincare and Infantasy for Five Celli
Concerto for Solo Violin and String Orchestra
Concerto for Solo Cello and String Orchestra
The Holy Sonnets of John Donne for Tenor and Strings

Arrangements
Cello Quartets
Cello Quintets

These works are available through
Shar Products Co.
PO Box 1411
Ann Arbor, MI 48106
(734) 665-3978

Byron Hoyt Music Co.
2525 16th St.
San Francisco, CA 94103
(415) 431-8055

Additional Compositions by Colin Hampton
Wisps for Four Celli (4 parts)
In Memoriam (4 parts)
Three Duos (2 cellos and piano)
Four Duets for Noah Guynn (2 parts)
Twelve Pieces for Twelve-Year-Olds (cello and piano)

Piano Pieces for Jessica Guynn
Seven Irritations for Two Girls and Two Cellos
Sonata in A Minor for Cello and Piano
Sonnet for Cello and Piano
Oreade for Cello and Piano
Vivace for Cello and Piano
Three Pieces for Cello Quartet
Songs, Vol. 1.
Songs, Vol. 2.
Five Whimsies for Two Celli (7 parts)
A Hymn to God, the Father
Three Sonatinas for Cello and Piano
Concertino for Cello and Orchestra
Two Chorals for Massed Cello
Sonata in E Flat for Cello and Piano
Two Viola Sonatas
Piano Sonata

Additional Arrangements by Colin Hampton
Anonymous: Over Hill and Dale (4 parts)
Bach: Praeludium XXII (4 parts)
    Salvation, Come to Earth (4 parts)
    O Lord, Our Father Forevermore (4 parts)
    Three-Part Inventions, Nos. 4 and 13 (3 parts)
    Ist ein allgemeines Lamento der Freunde (4 parts)
    Fugue No. 22 in B-Flat Minor (5 parts)
Beethoven: Cavatina from Op. 130 for String Quartet (4 parts)
    Slow Movement from Piano Sonata in D Major, Op. 28 (4 parts)
    Adagio from Op. 2, No. 2
Bloch: Meditation and Mah Tovu from Sacred Service (solo and 4 parts)
    Meditation Hebraïque (solo and 4 parts)
    Prayer (solo and 4 parts)
    Prelude (solo and 4 parts)

Corelli: Adagio (4 parts)
Dowland: Earl of Essex–His Galiard, from Lachrimae,
or 7 Tears (5 parts)
    Lachrimae Triste, from Lachrimae, or 7 Tears (5 parts)
    Lachrimae and Mr. G. Whitehead's Almand (5 parts)
Elgar: Nimrod, from the Enigma Variations, Op. 36 (12 parts)
    Variation No. 12, from the Enigma Variations (4 parts)
Fauré: Pavanne (5 parts)
Handel: Sonata Op. 2, No. 8 (5 parts)
    Larghetto, from Violin Sonata in G Minor (4 parts)
    Largo, from Oboe Concerto in G Minor (8 parts)
    Great Whales, from The Creation (5 parts)
    Theme and Variation from the Kaiser Quartet (4 parts)
Holst: Intermezzo from St. Paul's Suite
Jarnfelt: Berceuse for Cello and Piano
Lawes: Consort, Suite C Dur A6 (Fantazia) (6 parts)
Matheson: Air (4 parts)
Mendelssohn: Andante con moto from Italian Symphony (5 parts)
    It Is Enough, from The Elijah (5 parts)
Monteverdi: Lamento Della Ninfa (5 parts)
Mussorgsky: Scene 3 (March), from Khovanschina (5 parts)
    Scene 7 (Alla Marcia), from Khovanschina (4 parts)
    Serenade, from Khovanschina (6 parts)
    The Troubadour, from Pictures at an Exhibition (7 parts)
    The Ox Cart, from Pictures at an Exhibition (4 parts)
Paradies: Siciliano (4 parts)
Purcell: When I Am Laid in Earth, from Dido and Aeneas
    (solo and 4 parts)
Rossini: Sonata No. 3 in C Major, Slow Movement (4 parts)
Tschaikovsky: Legend (4 parts)
Franck, César, 7, 20

INDEX

OTHER TITLES FROM STRING LETTER PUBLISHING

21st-Century Violinists, Vol. 1, $12.95
An exciting collection of in-depth inverviews with the world's preeminent string players including Corey Cerovsek, Sarah Chang, Pamela Frank, Kennedy, Midori, Anne-Sophie Mutter, Elmar Oliveira, Nadja Salerno-Sonnenberg, Gil Shaham, Isaac Stern, and Maxim Vengerov.

Violin Virtuosos, $12.95
This fascinating companion to Vol. 1 includes profiles of Joshua Bell, Chee-Yun, Kyung-Wha Chung, Jorja Fleezanis, Hilary Hahn, Leila Josefowicz, Mark Kaplan, Viktoria Mullova, Vadim Repin, Joseph Silverstein, Christian Tetzlaff.

21st-Century String Quartets, Vol. 1, $12.95
In this collection of in-depth interviews, today's leading performers get to the heart of one of the most beloved forms of classical music: the string quartet. You are backstage with the American, Borodin, Emerson, Guarneri, Juilliard, Mandelring, Manhattan, Mendelssohn, Orion, St. Petersburg, and Tokyo String Quartets.

Musical Instrument Auction Price Guide, $44.95
Issued annually, illustrated with full-color plates of noteworthy instruments, the *Auction Price Guide* offers the most comprehensive information available on antique and handmade instrument and bow values. Asking and selling prices of instruments offered at the world's major auction houses are expressed in dollars, marks, pounds, and yen. A unique five-year summary by instrument and maker of high, low, and average prices shows market trends.

Commonsense Instrument Care Guide, $9.95
Violin maker and dealer James N. McKean, past president of the American Federation of Violin and Bow Makers, has written the essential reference on maintaining the playability and value of violins, violas, and cellos and their bows.

For more information on books from String Letter Publishing, or to place an order, please call Music Dispatch at (800) 637-2852 or fax (414) 774-3259, or mail to Music Dispatch, PO Box 13920, Milwaukee, WI 53213. Visit String Letter Publishing on-line at www.stringletter.com.